A PARENT'S GUIDE TO RAISING LEARNING-DISABLED CHILDREN

Jan Horner

ISBN: 978-0-578-43292-2

Printed by DiggyPOD, Inc., in the United States of America.

First printing, 2018

To my loving parents, Tom and Charlene Ruiter, my husband John and everyone who encouraged my dream.

Forward

As I read Jan Horner's extraordinary book "A Parent s Guide to Raising Learning-Disabled Children", I was constantly reminded of The Wizard of Oz. In this classic tale, Dorothy and her friends make a long, perilous journey searching for a powerful being to solve their problems and "bring them home".

Jan tells of her voyage to find answers to assist her kids as they struggled daily with learning disorders. Like Dorothy, Jan met several folks along the way. Some were helpful and supportive.... others were insensitive and hurtful. And — like Dorothy and her friends — Jan eventually learned that she actually had the power all along.

Jan's stories provide the reader with information and inspiration that can provide a parent or professional with valuable insights into the impact of learning disorders on the child and his family. This book will change your perspective on the day-to-day experience of kids who find 'school' a frightening and confusing place.

One of the greatest gifts that Jan gives the reader is her insistence that "one size does not fit all". She devotes a chapter to each of her children and the reader will see the wide variety of symptoms and challenges that are included under the wide umbrella of Learning Disorders.

I recommend that you take this journey with Jan. It will be an invaluable guidebook as you take YOUR journey."

Dr. Rick Lavoie

Introduction

I don't have a big degree from some huge university, (at least not yet); in the eyes of the world, I haven't accomplished greatness. I am not a self-made millionaire nor am I famous in any way.

So why would I write a book? I believe God has been preparing me for my whole life to write this book. He has blessed me with many unusual life experiences, and through them, I have learned a lot about what it takes to parent a learning-disabled child. What makes me qualified to write about this topic? Because not only do I have learning-disabled children, but I was one.

My unique life has struck me many times over the last couple of years. The first time occurred while taking a basic special education class. With each chapter we studied, my teacher would offer us extra credit if we had any experience in the current subject and wrote a short paper outlining the details.

Have you ever had a class where a fellow student always had something to say even if most of what they were doing was making things up to get attention? Well, I happened to be that student in this class, only I actually had all the experience I claimed I did.

I found that I knew the answer to almost every question the professor would ask. I had experience from raising my own children! God had given me many great experiences to learn from. My cousin Kiki once said,

"I've never really learned from what has gone right, but I always learn from the mistakes I have made." The same is true for me.

Last year during a conversation with an old friend, I realized that I had a unique perspective because of my varied experiences and that it was a gift. My friend was talking about dealing with the issues of her sister's child being disabled. It overwhelmed this family. She was thinking about how God could do this to her sister. I gave her a more positive way to look at the situation. She responded, "Where did you learn this stuff?"

I have an associate's degree in early childhood. She has a master's degree in business. I thought she was crazy to ask. I've only taken three classes dealing with special needs and none of the classes would have trained me to deal with family troubles. But as I will attempt to convey in this book, sometimes life is the best teacher of all.

Chapter 1

My parents and neighbors were great friends. They had a deaf and mentally-impaired son named Jimmy. Jimmy Kramer would ride his lawnmower over to my house every morning, take a seat at the table, and watch us get ready for school.

When I look back, I imagine he must've found it entertaining watching my mom get six children ready and out the door each morning. I grew up with Jimmy at our house, so I never considered it odd with him there. Until one day in first grade when my friend Mary spent the night with me.

In the morning Mary came upstairs when still getting ready for the day and said, "Jan, there's some weird guy in your kitchen. He doesn't talk!"

For the first time I thought about it; not everyone has a Jimmy at their house in the mornings. But my parents gave me that experience-that slight broadening of my horizon-because they loved Jimmy and didn't consider how he looked or communicated. Him being a part of our life was all that mattered to all of us.

Chapter 2

Just when my parents were confident they'd been through it all, there I was; always energetic and never sitting still. I can remember being told to stop fidgeting in church and feeling it almost impossible to do so, but Mom and Dad forced me to twice every Sunday.

I am now thankful for their perseverance. My Dad pulled me out more than a few times when I needed a little instruction. Mostly, they were tolerant of my legs wiggling through the whole sermon.

When I began Kindergarten, I was so excited and imagined it would be great; but by the end of the year, it became clear I wasn't as smart as the other children in my class. I did not catch on as quickly and although the other kids never picked on me; I felt like I didn't fit in.

In first grade, I knew I wasn't the smartest kid; but I would work so hard to make my papers look like everyone else's. I remember getting glasses in first grade, convinced they would work like magic and make me able to be like everyone else. No such luck.

My parents never let me use the word "stupid" or allowed me to pity myself. As long as I was doing my best, they were happy, and I knew they loved me.

By second grade, it became obvious I wasn't learning as quickly as others my age. My parents and teacher met, and she suggested that they should test me for a learning disability.

In the 1970s diagnosing and treating learning disabilities was still a new concept. The test results revealed that I had dyslexia. My parents attempted to explain that I was learning-disabled. They went to a clinic, where the director told them something simple. "Your daughter first needs to be taught that she can learn before she will learn," he said. And he was right. I believed in my head I was stupid and that me learning anything was hopeless.

He also said we needed to do three things: praise, repeat, and praise. We needed to find the positive. At first, my parents had a difficult time accepting this concept. I was content at home and had not shown signs of hating the whole school experience yet. I'm sure it confused them. How hard can life be at seven years old

However, the clinic director was right. At seven, I already felt overwhelmed. I'd given up, internalizing the fact that I was not smart. If they hadn't gotten help at an early age, it would have been a miracle if I had ever learned to read! When a child can't read, they become more dependent on others and life can easily bring them down.

It was during second grade when my parents held me back a year. This was really the best for me. It embarrassed me, but I sure fit in with the second group of children better than the first. Immaturity goes hand in hand with learning disabilities.

In my experience when kids are asked, most will say they dislike school. I was no different and I would often say I hated school. But fortunately, my classmates didn't mistreat me.

I remember trying so hard to be good at something. In first grade, the class was making life-size portraits of themselves for Parent's Night. I was working so hard at trying to be like everyone else. Someone commented "Wow! You are the only one trying to make it look real. We're all being goofy." I looked around and it was true. The other kids didn't see that this was my cover. I was hoping Mom and Dad would not notice how behind I was in the rest of the stuff!

That night my parents saw for the first time how I differed from most of my class. My bluff did not work. That same night they spoke with my teacher about what they could do to help me improve my learning skills.

It didn't take much for my parents to see that I was behind. They looked at my papers and compared them to the rest of the class. My dad pulled the teacher aside and said, "What do we do?" It relieved the teacher that she could talk to my parents and was thankful that they were receptive to her input and willing to do their part. They did not blame the school, themselves, or me. They faced the situation head-on: "Okay, what is next to help our daughter?"

Thus began a new chapter in my life. A new chapter that entailed hard work and new ways of learning. From then on until fifth grade, I went to the clinic every morning before school and even during the summer for special reading classes.

It felt like my mom was being mean forcing me to get up early before school to go to yet another school. I didn't even like school to begin with, so how could the solution be more school?

After school, I went to an eye doctor for exercises to help with eye control. I would have rather been home watching Speed Racer like the rest of the kids.

It's a family affair

My mom would work tirelessly for hours on end with me. She also recruited my sisters to play reading games with me. My sister Pat has many memories of working with me. She was always an easy learner. I think back and smile at the many times she played word games with me.

From my childlike perspective, the extra schooling was hard on me. Now that I am the parent of a dyslexic child, I realize just how much time it takes and I am grateful to my mother and siblings for their sacrifice.

I get my other children involved just as my mom did with me. I believe family has an inherent responsibility to help each other. I've received advice from my older children on how they would or would not handle the situation. I listen and give consideration to their thoughts, but more often than not I end up doing things my way.

Thinking back, I am increasingly awed at all my mom was able to handle. I was the youngest of six and my older siblings also had situations that my mother had to deal with. For example, one of my brothers rode a motorcycle up the high school stairs. Another one got a huge plastic cow on the top of the school building. My siblings were all creative! I am amazed to say I do not remember my parents getting overwhelmed by our teenage dramas. They seemed to have kept the bad influence of my siblings to a minimum.

I'm unsure if I was that self-centered and spacey or if my parents were that skilled at keeping me away from family drama. I am sure my parents kept the proverb, "Bring them up in the Lord and when they are old they will return," close to their hearts.

My parents encouraged repeatedly me by telling me that I was smart. My dad even told me that my dyslexia was a gift. He thought God had a plan for me and that I would become a great teacher for those who struggled like me. Like most teens feel at some point, I felt that my dad couldn't have been more wrong.

I didn't get a degree in education, but I can definitely see how God has taken dyslexia and made it work for my good in my life.

Proverbs 12:25 states that "Anxiety in the heart of man causes depression; however, a good word makes them glad." We need not have anxiety. We need to speak words of love. Doing this allows the children to process love and know they are wonderful the way they are.

A few of my older siblings struggled in school and rebelled against authority. I'm sure if my siblings and I went to school nowadays things would be different. There is more technology and knowledge available which makes learning easier.

Today, we are all blessed in so many ways that it's clear that God knows what He is doing and it's all in His timing, not ours. God has a perfect plan for each of us.

My parents made all that they did for us look like it was easy. It's important for you not to make your child feel as though they are a lot of work or that the extra cost of raising a child with disabilities is too much. My parents never complained about the extra bills it took to educate me.

My dad was a farmer who would never take government help and didn't care to rely much on insurance. To this day, he is a man of faith, that puts his trust in God before insurance and lawyers.

My dad trusted God to care for us. My mom doesn't recall how costly the clinic was, but she remembers being amazed continuously that God would make sure that all of our needs were met. All six of us went to Christian schools. Private schools were enough of a financial burden without the added cost of a child with special needs. It required a lot of prayer and faith in God.

Ultimately, I survived elementary school and junior high school. Fortunately, I didn't experience too much open rejection in my early years of school. However, I still realized that I did not comprehend everything like the rest of the class. I wanted so badly to fit in, but I was too immature to do so.

Confidence is key

I heard it said, "In order to succeed, your desire for success should be greater than your fear of failure." In second grade, when we figured out I was learning-disabled, I understood the math at the same level as everyone else in class. When I began the extra classes before school, I came to school late three days a week. This meant that I was missing my math classes.

This made me extremely behind in class. So much so, that one day, they gave me a paper with a multiplication sign on it, but I added everything because I thought it was a misprint. When my teacher returned the paper with all the wrong answers, I was too embarrassed to say anything.

I missed the introduction of the 'times' sign, just as I had missed other key elements in math. I also missed the chapter on how to tell time, and I still struggle with an analog clock. I was fortunate enough that my fourth-grade teacher noticed that I could not tell time. She would sit for hours working with me. My dad even stayed home from Sunday night church to work on it with me.

When I reminisce about schools in the seventies, I realize that back then; they did not know fully how to help children with learning disabilities grow to their full potential.

I always had trouble memorizing things. While in third grade, my teacher wouldn't move forward until everyone in the class had each verse memorized. I vividly recall that while learning the Lord's Prayer, my classmates were elated when I messed up because they didn't have to memorize more. One kid thought I did it on purpose to keep from learning the next Bible verse.

I still have a poor memory. I wish that I could memorize scriptures and retain them. When I cannot recall where a verse is just forces me to read the Bible more to find the verse. To every negative, there is a positive.

Today students with learning disabilities have more options like total inclusion, half day pull-out, or teacher aides in the classroom. There are differing opinions on the way to handle such students. I can see various difficulties with every method. Each child really requires individual solution. That is why students have Individual Educational Plans (IEPs) now.

I was done with special classes in fifth grade, which was a big transition year for me. It did not help that it was also my teacher's first year on the job. My teacher, Mrs. Krysheld told my mom she did not believe in learning disabilities. That poor woman didn't know what she was in for.

I do not know why the school hired her for the fifth-grade class. She ended up with a class full of the hardest children to teach. My mom talked to her a few times during the year but it was still a struggle. I had to write my name 3,000 times when I forgot my name on top of my homework. I remember my mom letting my siblings help write the names so I did not spend the whole weekend working through my punishment.

Mrs. Krysheld became so frustrated with a few of us in class she walked out of class crying the last day. But, ironically enough, a few years later she became an advocate for children with learning disabilities! Looking back, I was literally sick in the mornings before school for most of my fifth-grade year.

In seventh grade, I figured out my learning style. My English teacher, Mr. Hightsing, was normally the gym teacher; but an injury forced him in the classroom. He only knew me from gym class where I was actually decent. Perhaps it was because of that association it gave him more confidence in me than other teachers.

Instilling confidence is vital for getting them to learn. He did this by talking me into running cross-country. (I still enjoy running.) It's something he knew I would succeed in, and likewise, it was in his classroom that I really felt smart for the first time. It was also the first time I received an "A" in any class or schoolwork.

I don't know if Mr. Huitsing knew of the impact he made on me, but he exemplified an important quality you must possess when working with the learning-disabled: If you treat a child as though they cannot learn, they will not disappoint you. But if you give them confidence and a chance to soar, their success will be its own reward.

My Daughter's Drawing

Chapter 3

In the second year of high school, better grades became a habit. I came out of my shell and really believe in myself. I wish that I had graduated with a 4.0 GPA, but I'm proud to say I worked very hard for my B-minus average.

People diagnosed with ADD can be immature. Case in point, I was sitting on the school's back steps during my senior year when a friend asked me what I would do after graduation. I told him I would work at the farm stand again for the summer. Chris said, "No, I mean for the rest of your life."

I hadn't thought that far ahead. I did not have the confidence to even think about attending a university although I did eventually take several basic classes from the community college. I worked hard and surprised myself with A's and B's.

That's when it hit me-maybe I could do something with my life other than working at farm stands, which, when I thought about it; it held interest for me in the long term.

I might have been a late bloomer, but I believe was all in God's plan. Sometimes learning-disabled kids just need more time to build confidence before they are ready to face the world.

God will turn all things to good-Romans 8:28

God, (in His infinite Wisdom) knew my personal experience with dyslexia would give me the ability to persevere in life. Even when it seems the odds are against me, He gives me the ability to keep working and to continue moving forward.

Because of my experiences, I have the advantage of habitually thinking out of the box. If I could not learn something one way, I tried another. These were skills which proved useful when we lived overseas for a couple of years.

Having a learning disability also teaches you to ask for help. Admitting that you can't do it on your own is not a sign of weakness. In fact, it is actually a life skill that many never learn. Pride will often stand in the way of effective learning. When you can't learn without help, there isn't room for pride.

Now, years later, I'm still dyslexic-but have since learned that I have ADHD as well. This contributes to being extremely unorganized and having trouble staying on task. These are traits which can hinder me in life yet it gives me the unique ability to move from one task to another and gives me a great tolerance in chaotic situations.

In 1994, they gave my husband John an opportunity to move to Italy for his job. We jumped at the chance. When we moved, I adapted to the change fairly easily. Many mothers from the U.S. had a hard time adjusting to life in Italy.

When my kids started Italian school, the bus came between 8:00 and 9:00AM and school started around 9 or 9:30. The Lord blessed me with a laid-back attitude, so I could readily handle the change. In my disorganized approach to life, I was frequently late wherever I went in the United States, but in Italy; I was right on time.

Chapter 4

A good verse to remember is Proverbs 12:26 (NIV) "The righteous choose their friends carefully, but the way of the wicked leads them astray." When a child has no self-esteem, they will reach out to anyone to be their friend. Some of these so-called friends may try to lead them astray. To keep their confidence up, encourage your kids and try to help them find friends who love them for who they are.

The same applies to life partners. My husband John has given me more confidence than anyone else ever has. When you are learning-disabled, you need a fan club. I have experienced failure more than the average person. Without the enduring support from my husband and strength from family and friends who encouraged me to take on the world, I would never have made it to where I am today.

Low self-esteem

When you are learning-disabled, you may not have a high self-esteem . Thank goodness my parents had very positive outlooks. The worst comment I remember getting from Mom was, "If your head wasn't attached, you'd forget that, too." That was hardly a damaging blow. I have heard many horror stories of crushing comments made to a struggling child. Cutting remarks are not the only reason for low self-esteem. A proverb states, "the tongue can be sharper than a sword and far more damaging!"

My friend Julie told me her mother would say things like, "Oh, you forgot something. Do you know what forget starts with? An "F". Yes, an "F" just like the word failure." Talk about harsh words for a struggling child to process.

Similarly, my son Mike needed an MRI to make sure his inability to read was not being caused by some type of tumor. When the nurse came out of the testing room, she told me that Mike wanted fifty-one copies of his results. The nurse asked why he needed that many copies. Mike's response? He wanted to pass out the pictures to his classmates and siblings to prove that his brain was not the size of a peanut!

This tore at my heart but presents a real picture of how tough life can be for a child that is learning-disabled. Mike was young at this point but was already demonstrating how badly he wanted to fit in with his peers.

Sometime later my youngest daughter Amanda drew a cute picture of some squiggly lines. She showed me and said, "Mom, guess what this is!" It appeared to be an oval with a big bunch of spaghetti in the middle. In the center was a small circle. I said, "Is it a flower?"

"No Mom," she said, putting it on her head. "Look! Doesn't it look just like my brain?"
"Oh," I said.
"Yeah, it does."

Pointing to the small circle at the center she said, "This is my smarts." She was only in Kindergarten. That was an eye-opener for me. Children learn quickly the pecking order of supposed intelligence-who is smarter than whom. Even at age six, these things matter immensely.

Another reason that a child might have a low self-esteem is that even though they might actually be intelligent and just process things differently; when they hear the words "smart" and "good" and "gifted" they seem to apply only to other children. We hear the words "smart" and "good" and "gifted" when other children are described and assume that those words only apply to them.

Negativity is such a dominant factor when it comes to those who are learning-disabled. When I have to speak to a doctor about a negative aspect in my children's lives, I try not to have them present for the conversation. It always surprises me when a doctor will ask how their grades are in front of them as if they aren't there to feel the weight of the discussion.

Carol S. Dweck did a study in her book *Self-Theories: Their Role in Motivation, Personality, and Development* (Taylor & Francis, Inc., January 2000) that revealed that IQs can grow. She discovered that if you praised a child for work well done and let them believe their achievement was equivalent to being more intelligent, the child had improved capability of rebounding from the occasional failure.

I heard a little story about a group of frogs who climbed the tallest mountain. Everyone said they would never make it. A hundred frogs started up the mountain and along the way, people yelled to the frogs to stop-it would be too hard on them. Only one frog made it to the top. When they interviewed him, the reporter asked why he was the only one to succeed. Why didn't he listen to the naysayers and give up? Well, the frog was deaf. He hadn't heard a word of discouragement. He kept his focus on the task at hand, unaware that anyone thought he would fail.

The point is clear and relevant: Try your best to shield your child from words of negativity. They are far more damaging than you could ever guess.

Chapter 5

I have been so blessed with the many female friends with whom I can be open and honest with. They may not understand the specific dynamics of my life, but they support me and lovingly listen when I need to vent my frustrations.

Many are always ready with biblical advice too, which has helped to steer me through many trying situations. My sister Carol also has learning-disabled children. She has offered me invaluable advice and understands from experience the things I deal with daily. Many of which the average parent might freak out over. Carol does not judge or give inapplicable advice. She just laughs with me and offers needed support as I contemplate the specifics of my particular life, children and situations.

For example, the day I got a call from the school informing me that one of my sons had climbed the building. When I told Carol about it, she responded by telling me about her son's adventures and we shared a laugh.

When he came home, he said "Mom, you will get a call from school and I know it was dangerous to do. I know I'm not supposed to climb, but in my defense, I was bored and it's not my fault the builders made a perfect rock-climbing wall." He was joking.

Love, marriage, and LD

As a wife, I am not always easy to live with. I sometimes lose things and my house may not always be neat, but my husband John is always there encouraging me.

In all my searches through the Bible, I have never found a passage that says, "Cleanliness is next to godliness." I like to remind John of this whenever he gets on me about keeping the house up. I also remind him of the place in the book of Luke where Martha who was busy cleaning while her sister Mary who was sitting and listening at the feet of Jesus. (Luke 10:38-42) In that situation, who was doing the right thing? Jesus points out that Mary's priorities were straight.

This gives me hope. After all, if it were not an important factor, God would not have mentioned it in His Word. So, I feel better used by God to first spend my time listening to a friend or helping a neighbor, instead of worrying about keeping my house spotless.

If anyone needs proof that God has a sense of humor, look no further than my marriage. How John and I ended up together illustrates it perfectly. An extremely organized, super clean, a meticulous housekeeper and a fabulous cook raised John. To throw a wrench in expectation, God gave John me!

Without a doubt, I have been a factor in teaching John to have patience. And although my mother-in-law is as different from me as Mary was from Martha, we have a dynamic relationship.

John has been a blessing to me. He loves me-even with all of my crazy flaws. When we figured out I was also ADHD, I started on medication. The house was neater for a time, but I didn't like how the drugs made me feel. John likes the house to be neat, but he realized I wasn't happy. He lovingly hugged me and said, "I married you for who you are. Don't take the meds for me." So with his support, I stopped taking them.

It's vital to take medication for the right reason: to give the patient a better quality of life. In my opinion, medication shouldn't be used just to make life easier for others. For example; a child should not be medicated to relieve a mother or school's frustration, but rather, so the child can be better handle life without unnecessary and preventable stress.

Chapter 6

As I stated earlier, John and I have five children, (four are learning-disabled). Not one of our children learns the same as another. Each has his or her different strengths and weaknesses, like the children in any other family. However, I have been better equipped to parent learning-disabled children because I was one. They may have different weaknesses than I do, but I can still use nontraditional viewpoints. In my early years, it was from necessity, but it has become an invaluable strength nowadays.

Ephesians 6:4 says, "Fathers, do not exasperate your children. Instead, bring them up in the Lord." Having a child with disabilities can frustrate a parent, and it's easy to lose patience. But when you are parenting kids with disabilities, you need to take extra time to think as they do. Go into their world. For example, when you send an eight-year-old upstairs to change into pajamas, you may have to be clear with directions, and explain exactly which pajamas to put on and why.

Another way to help your learning-disabled child would be to only keep the current season's clothing and shoes available. Putting them away for the rest of the year removes unnecessary choices for your child to process and, ensures that they will not wear sandals in the snow or snow boots at the pool! It might be a good idea to make sure that flip-flops are hidden in the winter and, likewise, snow boots in the summer. Hiding them removed unnecessary information for my child to process and ensured I didn't have to worry about them wearing sandals in the snow or boots by the pool!   I know that this seems like a lighthearted example and may seem like a waste of time, but I can tell you from experience you need to be specific with instructions and remove distracting options like the wrong seasons clothing or you might end up losing your patience.

If you can't expect and eliminate distracting decisions and teach them how to do the same for themselves as they grow, you are allowing stress (on both of you) that is to be present that is wholly preventable.

Let me give you another example: Your child comes downstairs in the warm sleeper you didn't remove from the drawer. You shouldn't get upset because they were obedient. Don't yell when your little darling comes down the steps in the hot sleeper you knew was in the top drawer. They were obedient, but didn't have the broader sense of vision to realize the inappropriate choice of sleepwear.

Life as the parent of a learning-disabled child is a series of instances that will have consequences on your child's development. Your reaction determines one thing: will you help or handicap?

Chapter 7

It is hard when children first realize they are not learning at the same rate as others. They are perceptive enough to see that. In addition, they are usually aware of when they are being fed insincere praise and compliments.

A few years ago, John took our son Mike to a parent-teacher conference at his school. The math teacher had Mike mixed up with another student and told John that Mike was a top pupil in the class. John wanted to believe the teacher and never questioned it. A couple of weeks later Mike said, "I don't know how I have the best grades in class, because I get nothing right on my tests."

False praise, or insincerity in any form, is belittling. Praise your child for who they are, not for what you or others want them to be. If you can see that your child will fail at something, or may be overwhelmed, do what you can do to help them cope. Let them know you are proud of their effort.

I saw a bumper sticker that struck a chord with me recently: "God, please give me the patience to handle all of my blessings." I am far from the perfect parent. In fact, it would probably take another longer book to detail all the things I've done wrong. John and I try to learn from our mistakes, and I try my best to be one step ahead of my children. Try to learn from your mistakes. I try my best to think ahead of my children. However, no one can catch everything, and when embarrassing things happen, I try to only say encouraging things to my kids.

Devin

Our oldest was of course; the most wonderful baby ever born in the history of mankind. Everyone's firstborn is. We stared at him in wonder at the hospital, marveling over the sweet little thing God had given us. We named him Devin.

The doctor mentioned to John and I that Devin had yet to have a really good cry. As first-time parents, we didn't know what to do besides praying he would cry. Boy, was our prayer answered! Devin pretty much cried for two straight years until I took him to a natural doctor. Dr. Jennings was a chiropractor who worked with nutrition. He suggested we give him an all-natural diet, and he became a changed child. He finally slept at least four hours in a row! Another big change was that he did not cry throughout the day. He was at the doctor's at least once a month, but he was never sick again after his diet changed.

When Devin was about three, people shared concerns he might not hear as well as he should. We noticed that it was hard to get his attention. So, I took him in for two hearing tests-he failed both. I then took him into a specialist. She said she could see how he had failed the hearing test, but it was not because he could not hear. It was because he did not want to hear us. Dr. Bradley told me that Devin did not respond well to hearing tests, but when she started asking him about trains, he answered every question. At the time, my son lived for Thomas the Tank Engine. He even took a plastic train to bed with him at night.

Devin has learning disabilities we have never exactly pinned down. He struggled with many life skills, such as reading facial expressions, organization, and the ability to put his thoughts on paper. He now does well at all of these things. In fact, he is a wonderful poet and shows a good deal of wisdom for his age. He is also one of the best friends a person can have. He is kind and loyal to his friends.

Devin's inability to communicate well or respond was hard to explain. It wasn't stubbornness, but an inability to focus on more than one thing at a time. As he grew older, we could see that he had a lot of trouble following multiple-step directions. He struggled in new situations. He would get aggravated over things which were simple for his younger sister to comprehend.

When Devin started kindergarten, I came to pick him up and the teacher, Mrs. Teski, said he was having trouble listening to her. I questioned him about what happened. His response was, "Oh, you mean I have to listen to her like I listen to you?" It simply didn't occur to him.

He was well-behaved after that. Mrs. Teski was a wonderful kindergarten teacher. She used a different method to teach the letters. Each sound had a story to go along with it. She had the kids do very little actual writing but used picture clues for each sound and then had the kids add stamps of the letters themselves. Devin picked up the blending of sounds wonderfully because of this method.

As I mentioned previously, we moved to Italy for John's job. The first year there I home schooled Devin caught onto reading well with a lot of one-on-one time, but he struggled with writing. Because of this, I minimized his actual writing assignments. We used stamps and letter cards to spell and write. When he started the following year at his Italian school, he had a penmanship class and I assumed this would be enough to assist him with his writing skills. I also allowed him to move a lot. He was as hyperactive as I was. As long as he was learning why make him sit still?

I really was in denial that he was having trouble back then. In many ways, I was ignorant of the learning disability. I was teaching our next child, Jeannie, to write and read along with Devin. I thought that she was a genius. As it turned out, she was average. I just was so patient and did not realize how much work teaching my son required. We were fortunate that the Italian school he attended for three hours a day did not grade him harshly. Devin was doing fantastic in math.

The Italian schools were ahead of our American schools in math, so it was great to know the school in Italy was very encouraging for him. They knew the biggest reason we wanted him in school was for the exposure to other children and to help him learn the language.

Both Devin and Jeannie learned to speak Italian fluently. It was interesting to hear them speak. When referring to school, they spoke Italian, and when talking about home, they used English.

I did not realize how brave my children really were until we met another couple who were stationed there. The other family's children screamed when they first went to a school that spoke another language. It still impresses me how gung-ho my kids were to try anything thrown at them.

The problem came when we put Devin back in regular school. The class was not set up with him in mind-it was geared to typical learners. So we started doing three to four hours of homework at night.

It took a few years before I learned how to get help from the school. Devin worked so hard. Every night I would write every question and answer for him. I can remember once when he was in sixth grade, he said that he wanted to be an author when he grew up. I laughed to myself thinking how are you going to do that when I do most of your writing?" But he has definitely proven me wrong. He is now a fantastic writer and is very creative.

I've had to learn a lot of things the hard way. Getting help for my son was one hard lesson learned. The school initially assumed after testing him that he was just a little behind. They assumed it was because I had home-schooled him. Hindsight is 20/20, but I realize now that I should have questioned this assumption. If homeschooling was to blame, then why was my next child actually ahead in reading and writing? But I didn't question them.

After he struggled for two more years, I had him tested again by the school. His scores were now worse than before, so he started to receive services. I hoped that getting a little more help was all that he needed.

When Devin was tested, the teacher asked him to describe his life. He responded with, "My life is a blurry hurry. The only reason I know I have something else to do is because someone yells my name." The school was impressed with his visual description. But I felt so bad for him. I probably yelled or said his name 20 times while getting ready for school. It felt like I said it more than a hundred times a day. He felt controlled and helpless.

Medical help

The school suggested I take him to a doctor to explore his inability to focus. This particular doctor was a pediatrician and wrote out prescriptions before I could finish my sentences. I was trying to explain that Devin had a hard time dressing. Dr. Bob assumed that I was talking about an inability to follow through with directions. He wrote a prescription for ADD and an antidepressant for Devin to take before I had finished speaking.

We tried using these prescriptions, but it was a disaster. Devin had never been very chipper, but he became really down and had little ambition to play. He began speaking of suicide. That was an immediate cause for concern, so we stopped all medications after that.

Afterward, the school encouraged me to try a different

doctor or different medications. I refused to put him on any new medications without more thorough testing.

It was five thousand dollars to get him fully tested. Dr. Nowinski was thorough as she worked with Devin for a week. She gave a different diagnosis than that of the first doctor. We took the test results and diagnoses to the school and asked for a few more services. The school told us that Dr. Bob, and not Dr. Nowinski, were right, and we might want to reconsider the ADHD diagnosis.

At the time I was not as experienced with dealing with IEPs and the educational rights of children, so I let it go. Devin had a wonderful teacher, and I was not as worried about labels so much as I was about Devin's well-being and school life.

Contrary to what the school believed, Dr. Nowinski was right. She was a pediatric neuropsychologist. She gave me a lot of practical advice to help Devin. The results of that second batch of testing mirrored the concerns that I had for Devin.

He had a hard time remembering which direction shirts and pants went on, and he had tactile issues (he did not like the feel of certain fabrics). He had a hard time understanding other people's emotions as well.

When we went over the results, Dr. Nowinski said, "Your son must really have a hard time dressing." She also mentioned that Devin appeared to have sensitive skin. It was as if she was a fly on the wall and knew our struggles.

One piece of advice she gave me was to watch a movie with him but to stop in the middle and ask Devin what he thought the character was feeling. I used a James Bond movie. When I paused the film, the bad guy was being chased. I asked Devin, "What was the bad person feeling?"

His response floored me. He said, "Well, I think he is having fun. Look how fast he is driving. That would be fun."

The actor's face was full-blown fear. But Devin could not read facial expressions. We played this game often until he caught on to understanding facial emotions. The more I read about the disorder, the more I realized how much Devin really did not fit the label.

Chapter 8

But my second son Johnny did, and so did I. I took him to several doctors to find out what to do. Sure enough, he was diagnosed with ADHD. He started medication when he was in first grade. It was not easy on me to start medication this time around. It terrified me that he would spin into depression just like Devin.

This time, however, we had great results. We had more testing done and found another new doctor. Johnny's IQ went up by quite a few points, mainly because he could finally focus on the testing. Johnny was also very creative and hyperactive. He learned his multiplication tables by being allowed to do flips off the couch if he got them right. As a byproduct, three years later he took second place in state in gymnastics!

Johnny struggled similarly as Devin, but not all the same. Once again, I learned different ways to get him help within the school system. The first step in that process was diligence in documenting all of my concerns for the child. Two "problems" which we had to deal with actually turned out to be two of Johnny's best traits-creative thinking and an independent nature.

Johnny was never afraid to be himself. When he went to a kindergarten, it was obvious the first day that school would not be easy for him. First, he told me to just drop him off at the door. I was surprised. At the age of six, he didn't want his mother with him. I said, "It's your first day away from me, I'm walking you in."

"Okay," he said, "but do not cry."

He was so independent. But when he came home, he said he wasn't going back.

"Why not?" I said.

"Didn't you like it?"

"That was the dumbest place I have ever been. The teacher gave us all the same paper and said to color it the same way. Doesn't she know that there are copiers in the office?"

In Johnny's eyes, those repetitive tasks were silly. He was very intelligent. He needed to know why he was required to do a task. To conform, to be just like everyone else, was silly to him.

He still thinks this way today. In his mind, the school had a bias and he considered it oppressive and impeding to his creativity and independence.

It's easy for me to believe there are many children who feel the same. One can understand that school is set up with a structure for a very good reason. They are trying to teach a large group of students, and it is not possible to instruct each child individually. So those with different learning styles can easily feel they don't belong.

It is important to let kids know that it is not wrong to think outside the box. Those who aim to conform will probably never make history or excel beyond the norm. Those who think outside of the box are the catalysts of change that our future may depend on for answers. How exciting!

In fact, God makes it clear that standing out is what He wants us to do. In Jeremiah 1:5, He says that He sets us apart. Yes, we are set apart as Christians in a secular world-but even more so, we are to be set apart as the dynamic individuals that He created us to be.

We must make our children aware that while they can be proud of who God made them to be, they must not be full of pride or disrespectful about it.

This seems to be an ongoing challenge with Johnny. He was fed up when taking the three-year review test and decided to mess with the teacher's head while she was administering it. When I went to the meeting to get the results, I was shocked at how concerned she was about him. She said that he did not smile enough and that he had an eating disorder. He seemed to be obsessed with cheese.

Another teacher, Mrs. Lofton, who understood Johnny, looked at me and said, "Johnny just played with that lady's head." I had to laugh because she was right. When I got home, I told Johnny that I had an interesting meeting at the school. He smiled and said, "Does the teacher think I love cheese?" I asked why she thought that he didn't smile enough, and he replied: "She was not funny. Besides, why would I smile? It was school."

You cannot force a child love school. My son loves learning, but not the institution of school itself. It followed him from one grade to the next. Each year the school would document his refusal to conform.

Once it was a concern that he didn't have a consistent set of friends to sit with for lunch. But they didn't understand that Johnny had made it a game. He would purposefully sit at a different table every day. Monday was one table, followed by a different one on Tuesday, Wednesday, and so on.

At each table, he would sit and say, "Today you're my best friends." He made up new names for everyone at each table as well as each person that rode his bus. He never had any problem remembering each new name. It seemed that what he was actually doing was making fun of the social system.

Contrary to what the school personnel thought, Johnny had and continues to have friends. He's just not as much of a social person and becomes uncomfortable in group situations. My other children would've loved the invitations he turned down. This concerned the school, and at one point I was required to take him in for physiological testing. It was devastating to his self-esteem. I took him to see three different doctors. All reviewed his case, and all felt that he was a classic ADHD-not emotionally-disabled.

The medication prescribed to some of my kids really works for them. When they can focus, they do well in school. It also helps them control their impulses. I think the impulsiveness of ADHD is the hardest part to manage. People think it's just an excuse for bad behavior.

Admittedly, it's hard to figure out how much of the kids' bothersome urges is the ADHD and how much is them just being themselves.

It's a fine line and decisions regarding an ADHD child are not all black and white. For example, it's a learning process to know when to punish a child and when not to. As with any other aspect of parenting, it is a process of learning along the way.

Chapter 9

Our fourth child named Mike also gave us experiences which helped us to grow and learn as parents, just as his other siblings did. When he was born, Mike has webbing over part of his voice box-a condition known as "webbed larynx" He came two weeks past due with the umbilical cord was wrapped around his neck. He was blue and had to spend a short time on oxygen. For John and I, it felt like hours.

Even with these early challenges, we were able to bring him home after only two days. I observed that his cry was weak, but the nurses told me to stop worrying. After a week of no crying, I took him back in and insisted that they listen to his cry. The doctors knew we were soon moving back to the United States and suggested that we see a specialist. It was clear that something was wrong, but because he ate well and he had no difficulty breathing they weren't terribly concerned.

Back home, Dr. Mail took a scope and looked down Mike's throat. Dr. Mail told us about the larynx webbing and that Mike would need surgery when he was around 18 months old. Before the surgery, he only knew four words.

He had the surgery, but Dr. Mail told us to start learning sign language because the webbing was much thicker than he had expected. They simply weren't sure whether Mike would ever be able to speak, and if he did start to produce sounds, they would probably be raspy-like Froggy from *Little Rascals*.

So we taught him sign language. The first thing Mike learned to sign well was "more cookies" and "more milk." This is still one of his favorite snacks.

Once again, the doctors were wrong. With a lot of prayer and help from a speech therapist named Rita, Mike actually learned to speak! His voice wasn't raspy either, but turned out to be more high-pitched. When he was young, he would belt out the Sunday school songs like no other child in the choir. It made many of us who had prayed for him smile.

Because Mike's speech was so delayed, the rest of his brain processing was late as well. He had in-home therapy until age three and went to a special education preschool after that. We would work on counting and writing his name over and over again and thought we'd done everything we could. But when he started school, he was still behind his first two years. The school kept telling me that it was immaturity and that soon things would start clicking, and he would learn.

Mike struggled socially. He tried so hard to make friends with other kids that he ended up scaring them away. There were even times when I saw him mistreated by other children.

When we met with his teacher in the middle of Mike's second grade year, I was concerned because I felt Mike was not really learning. Mrs. Gordon, whom I adore to this day, tried to assure me that while Mike was in special education; he was that far behind the other children in the class. She felt that he was reading at a 1.3 level. I then asked to have his reading tested, and the school agreed.

We had a meeting to discuss the results, and his teachers and therapists gave their thoughts about Mike's learning style and ability. He did, in fact, test at a K-1 level, which meant that he had a few letters, but no phonic sounds or sight words. But he was going into third grade.

It might seem confusing that parents or teachers could be unaware how far behind he was, but I can tell you that when you want to believe so badly that your child is okay, that they can read but maybe they're just a little behind, it is easy to not grasp the full reality. You want to believe what the teacher is telling you.

As for his teacher not knowing, one possible explanation is that Mike would memorize what he heard and what he was supposed to read. When it came time for him to read, he would simply recite what he had memorized. For a time, it worked.

I questioned Mike's reading ability when I noticed that he was changing the order of the words, saying, "Grandma said" instead of "said Grandma." The class method was for each child to read one small paragraph a week, each one a part of a larger story. Mike just memorized the section that he was supposed to read, and no one knew.

When all the reports were given, Mrs. Goedke, who was running the meeting, turned to me and said, "We are working as hard as we can. Now we need your help."

I was shocked. I could not believe that the school was insinuating that I was not doing my job when I had always been the one pressing for more testing and asking for more help. They said that I needed to send him to school with no stains on his shirt, and to always send his glasses. They thought if that was done, then he would be able to focus on schoolwork and be able to learn to read. Their accusations surprised me-upset me, actually. "So you're saying that we're not going to do more or change anything in school for the next year?" I said.

After some debate, they agreed to try to get him one-on-one time with a teacher for 20 minutes a day. I was driving home from a trip to Chicago after the meeting, in the middle of messy traffic, and I realized the school was essentially pinning Mike's reading disability on me. On top of that, they weren't planning to do much more to help him.

Then it struck me-it was right in front of me, and I missed it. It was in front of the school, and they missed it too. Comment after comment was made in that meeting about how Mike had put his shoes on backwards too often. How he still could not tie his shoes and struggled with the difference between right and left. I was even told that he had argued with the principal over whether the number 9 was a letter 'P.' How could I have missed it when, like me, he was clearly dyslexic? He had the same problems that I did! I felt like a failure as a mother-it should've been so obvious.

I calmed down a little and called the principal the next day. But I let go a string of accusatory words-how dare they miss this; how dare they blame the mother. I spoke tough for about two minutes and then realized that my phone had dropped the call. The phone began ringing. God has a funny way of helping us out in moments of weakness.

I answered and asked the principal, "How much of that did you hear?"

"It cut out at the word how," she said.

"Well, I didn't swear," I said, "but I don't know if I was respectful before."

Then we had a nice conversation about getting Mike the help that he needed. She was very gracious and apologized if she hurt my feelings at the first meeting.

Ultimately, John and I tried homeschooling him for the next year. Throughout the summer, I worked with Mike. We had a third set of testing done at Rush University. Mike worked for over seven hours on a test which normally takes a learning-disabled child four hours. It was also October 31. Mike desperately wanted to go trick-or-treating later that afternoon.

We sat down with Dr. Bryan Bernard, Ph.D., (a clinical neuropsychologist) who confirmed that Mike was learning-disabled. My thoughts were, "Okay-I knew that much." Dr. Bernard said he had never seen a child work so hard and so long with a smile on his face. Through it all, Mike never gave up.

I taught Mike at home for a year. We went to eye therapy and a dialectic specialist. I felt good about Mike's progress. It was very slow but steady improvement. At that point, he had picked up nineteen sight words and was at a 1.1 reading level.

As far as I knew, the homeschooling was an improvement over public school. Even so, there was more that he needed-more than we were not able to give him from home. There was more technology at school, I felt Mike would benefit from more movement in his day. But at that time, we were doing the best that we could, and I could see a positive change.

This was such a hard decision. We had asked another opinion from a school principal near our house. The principal had reviewed Mike's tests and suggested that we continue to home school.

Harsh reality

As I home schooled Mike, we had a lot of one-on-one time. As time went on, he revealed, bit by bit, how horrible school had been for him the year before. He talked about his fear of letting people know he could not read and some mean names they had called him.

Whenever he would tell me what one of the bullies said, he would finish with, "Oh, but don't tell their moms-they were just joking." I was shocked to learn that one of the kids being mean to him was the son of one of my good friends!

It's an odd situation to be in. He wanted to belong so badly. It broke my heart. I never told the other parents because it was over and in the past. In addition, the other children just did not understand. Boys will be boys, so I let it go.

I tried to keep in mind a conversation I had with Devin several years earlier. He came home from school with bruises. I asked him where the teachers were at when he was getting beat up on.

Devin replied, "Mom, kids are not stupid. They wait until a teacher isn't looking." It was a good point. With just five children, I don't know everything that happens in a day so I can see how the children get away with it when there are 20 to 30 kids to manage at once. But teachers need to be aware of kids who are picking on the others.

How reading affects everything

I finally realized how much not being able to read was affecting my son one Sunday morning at church. The minister asked the congregation if they knew what a billboard near the church had written on it. It was an advertisement for the movie *The DaVinci Code*. The answer was the word truth.

Mike loved being in the spotlight and speak out in church. I told Mike the answer, but he didn't want to speak. When I asked why, he said he was afraid that Pastor Mark would ask if he had read it, and said, "Then I'd have to say no, and everyone would know I can't read." Not knowing how to read is a pressure at any age.

One of the most embarrassing moments that Mike had to deal with was when a friend happened to be wearing a hat that had a simple word on it. My friend who was unaware of the reading issue, said, "Hey-what does this say?" He happened to say it very loudly in a crowded room. Mike said, "I can't read it." It was a terribly awkward situation.

Needing to do more

John and I took all the testing results we had done, along with all the documentation from the various doctors, and went to the school for an IEP meeting about Mike. Ultimately the principal suggested that we consider an alternative school option, which we did.

Not only was it a great new school, but it was also a Christian institution. John wanted us to tour the school before making a final decision, so we scheduled a visit. The school's name was Elim Christian School. It was about 45 minutes from our house.

On the way to the school, I was trying to get John to see the favorable side because to me it sounded like the perfect solution, but he felt hesitant. However, when we walked through the school, to my surprise, I was the one backing out. Something in me didn't feel right, and I wasn't sure this was where I wanted to send Mike.

I saw children had bigger challenges than Mike. The other students might have had the same IQ, but they were in wheelchairs. Some of them could only speak through sign language. What were we doing? We didn't want Mike to think less of himself.

I sat and cried, but John was the strong one. He wasn't entirely sure either, but we really saw no other alternative. We prayed it was the right choice. We were certain that he would feel loved there, and that he would receive more than I could give him on my own. It was a tough decision to make. Part of me felt that I was letting him down by not homeschooling him any longer. I was terribly afraid that he would lose his self-esteem.

But despite my fears, we ended up sending him, and it turned out to be a great decision. He loved it there. It was a wonderful feeling to go on parent night and see that he was learning at the same rate as everyone else.

That doesn't mean it was easy to begin with. When we told Mike that he was going to attend there, the first thing he asked was, "Do you think I am retarded?"

As you can probably imagine, it was a very difficult discussion to have with our child. Disabilities are hard concepts for adults to comprehend, let alone children.

Explaining to his siblings why Mike was going to be

attending a different school was also difficult. We talked to them individually, and they each had a different reaction.

Now, years later, we are still struggling with, Mike's self-esteem issues. Mike loves his school and his friends there. Yet he doesn't want anyone outside of his school world to know that he goes to Elim.

It's a constant prayer for John and I that Mike will feel good about himself. He's somewhat caught between two worlds-those who have disabilities that are visually obvious, and those who have disabilities that can't be seen.

Finally, our last child Amanda was born. She seems to be THE happiest child on the earth. She wakes up every morning singing even though she too struggles in learning. Her speech was delayed, but her large motor skills are great. I thought her small motor skills were excellent as well before I had her tested.

I assumed her small motor skills were good because she is and always has been an artist. She may be able to stay in the lines and sketch out her thoughts brilliantly, but she couldn't copy any letters or shapes easily. She has an incredible wit yet doesn't have the ability to follow simple directions.

Amanda had the advantage of being our last. We are now armed with the knowledge of recognizing signs having a learning disability, so I was able to make sure she got help right away. We started with home-therapy at two years old, and then Mandy went to a special needs preschool at age three.

One of the most difficult aspects to deal with was potty training. She was four and a half when she was finally done. Amanda would cry when I put a diaper on her when we went out because it made her feel like a baby. It was highly embarrassing for her, but she just couldn't control it.

I worked with her, and we did the best that we could to manage. One of the hardest things was the looks we got from other people. Many would comment on her lack of potty training and even accused me of failing to do it. As if we weren't trying. I felt like responding with, "Oh, well, actually I love changing dirty pants so much that I just want to keep her in diapers until she's eight!"

One of the worst suggestions I ever heard was to spank her after every accident and then make her change her own pants. I had just finished explaining that Amanda was developmentally delayed. Of the seven children in my daughter's class, only four were potty trained. When there are prevailing delays in learning, it's natural for other areas to fall behind as well.

Trust me, I wanted to say, if spanking her for an accident would have fixed it, then all the mothers of this class would have tried it. No one looks forward to changing the dirty pants of a three-year-old.

Before Amanda went to kindergarten we had testing done, so that we were more aware of what we would be

facing. And so far, the school has done a wonderful job working with her. It's incredibly important to make sure that we were on the same page as the school.
It was hard, but we tried a few medications to help her focus. It was very scary putting a six-year-old on drugs.

We are waiting until Amanda gets a little older before we work with auditory processing and vision ability. Both tests show that she is behind in these areas but the doctors feel she isn't ready to work with these areas yet. If she can't focus, the therapy will do little good.

It is frustrating for me to see her struggle because she is intelligent in so many ways. When she was younger, Amanda shared a room with Jeannie, who is 13 years older, and at night Jean, would write in her diary. Amanda was four years old when she asked Jean why she wrote every night. She explained that she was detailing the big things in her life.

A week later, we found a book under the bed with drawings of events from that year. Each drawing showed emotion-some happy memories, like fishing with Dad, but others of traumatic events, like a house fire we'd had a year earlier. The picture was scary. How could a four-year-old grasp the concept of putting emotions on paper without knowing her colors?

There was another situation a few years later, which also ripped my heart out. Amanda was seven, and we were looking at a picture from my wedding day. She was picking out different people that she knew, and when she came to Barry, a friend of ours, she said, "Oh, I like this guy. He has no mean brain of me."

"What do you mean, 'no mean brain'?" I said.

Mandy looked at me and said simply: "He does not think I'm stupid."

Barry has been a family friend for years as he's married to Diane, one of my good friends. He often teases Mandy playfully. As soon as Mandy got on the bus that morning, I called Diane. She said, "Oh, I'll tell Barry. That's so cute."

"Yes, it is sweet," I said, "but you don't really understand what this means to me.

There are many people who Amanda feels unwanted around. My kids have been told negative things openly. They have seen me talked about negatively. Some kids can let it roll off their shoulders, but Mandy is very sensitive.

"It's a wonderful thing to know that she is welcomed and loved just as she is in your home." I couldn't help but cry tears of joy as I told this to Diane.

There are moments when it's hard for me not to panic. I don't want Amanda to have to struggle the way my other kids have. Getting her help as early as possible was the best thing we could've done for her.

Almost immediately, she knew that she was not learning like the other kids in her class. The biggest challenge has always been to keep her focused on the positive and reinforcing the fact that she is smart.

Chapter 11

Every parent-to-be has initial dreams of having their son or daughter end up as the prom queen or the valedictorian. It's normal. Everyone thinks their kids are the most wonderful beings to be brought into the world.

For many children, disabilities are obvious from the beginning. But less severe ones take years to show their effects. Still, some parents are in denial and don't recognize what's before them. Others blame themselves because their child is not the straight-A student or the social king.

I've often thought of the image of teenagers that are presented in movies. In our home, Troy Bolton is a prime example. If you have seen the *High School Musical* movies, then you know Troy has dilemmas-should he spend time with his high school friends or the college scout who is offering a scholarship? Should he go to Juilliard or a state school?

I wish my kids' decisions were on that level. Instead, many parents fear their children will have too many days like *Napoleon Dynamite*-getting beat up for lunch money and harassed because they don't run with the "in" crowd.

When I get overwhelmed with these thoughts, it's good for me to remember what Psalm 139:14 says about the beauty of individuality:

"I praise you because I am fearfully and wonderfully made..."

God does not make mistakes, nor is He ever surprised. He did not accidentally give you a random child to raise. You and your child were paired together for a reason. You are the perfect match.

I think it takes the pressure of knowing God does not care how organized you are. He doesn't care about looks or even grades. We are to train our children up to be holy, not just valedictorians. We need to be a model of what holiness looks like and make sure they know God has a plan for them. He desires us to give our best, not necessarily to be the best.

Chapter 12

So many people are ignorant of what a learning disability is. These are the criteria (Federal Reference 1977, P. 650 Nichcy):

Academic difficulty: the child with learning disabilities has a difficult time learning to read, spell, organize thoughts, or do mathematical equations compared with children of the same age.

The discrepancy between potential and achievement: the child with learning disabilities experience serious discrepancy between intellectual ability and achievement in school. This is known as an aptitude-achievement discrepancy.

Exclusion of other factors: A person may not be classified as having a learning disability if there is a learning problem caused by visual or hearing impairments, mental retardation, motor disabilities, emotional disturbance or environmental factors.

Neuropsychological disorder: Basic learning disabilities result from some type of neurological disorder. I remember reading an article that claimed that doctors can literally see a difference in brain mass on MRIs of children who are dyslexic versus those who are not.

Here are thirteen different disabilities according to the Individuals with Disabilities Education Act (IDEA):

1. Autism
2. Deaf/blind
3. Deafness
4. Emotional disturbance
5. Hearing impairment
6. Multiple disabilities
7. Orthopedic impairments
8. Other health impairments
9. Specific learning disability
1a. Speech or language impairment
11. Traumatic brain injury
12. Visual impairments
13. Mental retardation

The academic disabilities are usually grouped into four disorders:

1. Language and Reading Disorders
2. Mathematical disorders
3. Deficits in executive functions
4. Memory disorders

Language and reading disorders

A language disorder is a general term referring to difficulties in listening, speaking, phonetic mastery, word recognition, reading, spelling, and writing. Dyslexia, dysgraphia, and spelling disorders fall under this category. (See Lyon 1994, 1999, Okolo, Cavalier, Ferretti, and MacArthur, 2000 for more detail.)

Dyslexia usually refers to a severe reading disability involving difficulties in understanding the relationship between letters and sounds. Dysgraphia is an inability to perform motor movements and can be characterized by extremely poor handwriting. Spelling disabilities can mean that the person can read fine but have an inability to remember how to spell words from memory.

Mathematical disorders
Mathematical disorders or dyscalculia refer to selective impairments in mathematical thinking or calculation skills.

Deficits in executive function
To be able to learn in the ways that the school presents learning, children must be able to master skills known as executive function, metacognition, or cognitive strategies. These are internal processes that a child must use to select, control, and monitor in order to learn.

Memory disorders

These can be a deficit in short or long-term memory.

Other health impairments

ADD and ADHD are categorized here. ADD is a pattern of inattention that is frequently displayed more severely than is typically observed in individuals at comparable levels. ADHD is the inattentiveness with hyperactivity.

It's important (and can be frustrating) to understand that several disorders have overlapping symptoms that can give false diagnoses. It is vital to have a correct understanding of the child's individual condition so that the proper treatment and assistance can be obtained.

To make things more complicated, there are many learning problems such as memory, perceptual motor, or visual processing deficits which give us more to work on.

Why are the right diagnoses so hard to acquire? If one's leg is broken, an X-ray can be done to verify the break. It is not the same with learning disabilities. Many of them have similar symptoms. In addition, many children have more than one disability, which makes sense-if one part of the brain is struggling, it would have an effect on other parts.

When a child has a disability, it means one thing: he or she has a disorder. They are not stupid, nor are they lazy. Many times, these kids work harder than the children without disabilities and still end up with a lesser result. These learning-disabled children are intelligent, and they need help and encouragement, just like any other student.

How do we know?

What's the difference between a delayed learner and a learning-disabled student? Learning-disabled students' scores show that they have the potential to be doing the same work as their age-based peers, yet their product is behind that of the other students.

A delayed or slow learner can be the product of a poor environment or other things holding the child back. If a child is blind, it is obvious to teachers and the rest of the world he or she is visually impaired. People don't need a document to prove that. But that is not the case in the learning-disabled world.

Understanding the nature of learning disabilities is the first step as a parent. Read books to become informed. Realize that being learning-disabled is not just a disability in the classroom. It affects every area of life-educational and personal.

The reaction

Families that discover that their child has a disability may have a variety of reactions. These responses may run a gamut of emotions:

Denial

This was my first reaction, which really was more ignorance than anything else. I could see that one child learned easier than another, so I felt it was a difference, not a problem that needed addressing.

I was not in denial after we received a diagnosis. I was very relieved, because we couldn't start to treat a problem until we know what's causing it. John, on the other hand, not having the life experience with learning disabilities that I do, was probably more in denial than I was.

Not all parents go through denial. One parent I spoke to knew from the day she brought her baby home that there was something wrong, and she was relieved to receive a diagnosis. Unfortunately, she had to deal with the denial of other people in her life. Extended family, such as grandparents or aunts and uncles.

Sometimes denial is the result of ignorance, but many times it is a result of dealing with the harsh reality that sometimes people just don't want to face the fact that their child has a disability.

One of my friends, who has a background in special education, has a son who was born with many physical impairments, including the need for heart surgery. She knew he was going to be a special case.

Her husband was very much in denial were many others in their life. People would tell her not to worry about her son. They would say she was just concerned because of the job she has that she's going to assume that everyone has problems. "Not every child will have developmental delays, you know," is a comment that she heard a lot.

I can understand her frustration. Once in a while, I have seen signs of learning disabilities in the children of my relatives, but if I would ask them to keep an eye out for it, my insight would not be happily received.

Dealing with the denial of others is difficult. You can feel that they are not taking you or your child seriously, and when it's your son or daughter's future at stake, it's a tough pill to swallow.

Anger

The anger I experience is probably at myself. Parents don't want to see their child suffering as I did as a child while trying to learn to read.

Some can also feel anger at their spouse, fearing that learning disabilities are genetically transferred. Many might also feel angry at God because other parents don't have to deal with these trials. A few of the parents with whom I've talked say they are a little angry at God or just "life." And in these situations, it's easy to adopt a "why me?" attitude.

Fear

Facing the fear-the reality-of what all this can mean is huge. I feared for my children socially. When they hurt, I hurt. I feared they wouldn't learn well enough to fill out an application at McDonald's. I feared they would face lifelong battles with thoughts of feeling rejected and unwanted.

Some other parents I talked with said they were afraid that they were not going to be able to afford the doctors their children needed to get appropriate help. One father said he felt horrible because the basic needs of his child could not be met with his weekly paycheck.

Guilt

I am naturally a guilt-driven person. I feel guilty and somewhat responsible that Mike is having similar problems I did, which is silly. Do I really feel guilty for birthing my children? Of course not. I am thrilled with each of them, and they have all been wonderful in their own special ways.

Other mothers said they feel guilty because they had a hard time carrying their children during pregnancy. What if they did something wrong while they were pregnant? What if they were too stressed or not eating well enough? What if they actually did something to bring this on their child?

I've talked to others in the same situation as me: a father or mother with disabilities. They all go through the same thoughts or feel guilty that their children inherited this from them. But their kids inherited good things, too. And if we teach our children to see the positive, they can recognize the good in their lives and can use the disability to bring honor to God.

I recently heard Brad Cohen speak. He's a teacher with Tourette's Syndrome. He has published a best-selling book and has had a movie made about his life. When he was ready to have his first child, he said, "Who better to parent a child with Tourette's than me?" He was aware there was a 50 percent chance that his son would be born with Tourette's Syndrome. in the same way, I think: who better to raise an ADHD child than me?

Confusion

It's difficult to balance the sheer number of choices and decisions that have to be made such as: Which doctor, which medications do we use, should we pursue all-natural treatment? Do we change schools, get extra tutoring? And the list goes on.

Disappointment

No one wants to face more work. Everyone wants their child to succeed in life. But we can't feel disappointed in the children God gave us, only the situations we must deal with. There is a difference.   Some parents I have spoken with have told me they went through a grieving period when their child was diagnosed. They felt they had lost the child they were meant to have.

One mother grieved that her son would never have the life he deserved. Her oldest son had been captain of every team he'd ever joined. And now she worried that her second would miss out on all of his achievement opportunities.

These emotions are natural reactions and are perfectly normal in the face of an unexpected situation. But once a parent processes through their feelings, it's very important to understand that there is a purpose behind everything, to find contentment in even the most difficult situations (Ecclesiastes 3:1-8)

As a mom, it is easy to feel it is my job to make the house happy. I plan the birthday parties and buy the Christmas presents. Happiness is a state of mind, and it is impossible to make another person feel happy. I can't find any Scripture commanding believers to be happy, although there are references stating the Lord enjoys it when we are happy in God himself (1 Timothy 6:17, Nehemiah 8:10, Psalm 35:4, Psalm 98:12, John 15:11).

The first step to happiness is contentment. Hebrews 13:5 says, "Keep your lives free from the love of money and be content with what you have because God has said 'I will never leave you or forsake you'."

Contentment is a learned process, one that is hindered by comparing your child with others. Not every child is made the same-every child's intelligence isn't going to be the same either. It is a damaging process to compare one child with another.

It's like an illustration I once heard: A person is very happy eating his medium ice cream cone. Until he sees another person who has a bigger cone with an extra scoop of vanilla. Then suddenly, his isn't enough. He wants more, better, different.

But contentment isn't promised in life, nor is equality or fairness. Contentment is being grateful and satisfied with what God has given you.

In Philippians 4:12, Paul says that he knows what it is to be in need, and what it's like to have plenty. He has learned the secret of being content in any situation, whether well fed or hungry, whether living in plenty or in want. Then he says in verse 13, "I can do all things through Christ who strengthens me." Jesus is pure contentment. We need no more than this.

As a parent, it is important to learn contentment. If I show a lack of contentment, my child may feel a burden. How can I expect my child to possess a quality if I do not? It is harder to see the blessings around us if we are blinded by ungratefulness, frustration, or comparisons, and we may not ultimately be used by God for His purposes.

Signs to look for-Birth to preschool

1. Crawls late
2. Speaks later than other kids
3. Pronunciation of syllables
4. Slow vocabulary growth
5. Inability to find the right words
6. Difficulty rhyming
7. Trouble learning basic lists (days of the week, numbers, letters, colors, shapes)
8. Extremely restless or easily distracted
9. Trouble interacting with other peers
10. Difficulty following directions
11. Slow developing fine motor skills
12. Slow developing large motor skills
13. Overly sensitive to touch, texture, sound, or light

Signs to look for-Grades K through 4

1. Slow connection between letters and sounds
2. Confuses basic words
3. Makes consistent reading or spelling errors
4. Left and right confusion

5. Slow to learn new skills

6. Relies mostly on memorization

7. Substitutes words (such as house for horse)

8. Poor organization

9. Poor   pencil   grip

10. Trouble learning to tell time

11. Poor coordination

12. An unawareness of physical surroundings

Signs to look for-Grades 5 through 8

1. Reverses letter sequence (soiled for solid)

2. Difficulty with handwriting

3. Holds writing utensils with an abnormal grip

4. Avoids writing

5. Slow to learn prefixes, root words, and other spelling strategies

6. Avoids reading out loud

7. Trouble recalling details

8. Difficulty making friends

9. Trouble reading facial expression

Signs to look for-High school and adult years

1. Continues to have difficulty spelling, including spelling the same word differently

2. Avoids writing and reading tasks

3. Trouble summarizing things

4. Difficulty with open-ended questions

5. Weak memory

6. Difficulties in new situations

7. Works slowly

8. Poor grasp of abstract concepts

9. Pays too little or too much attention to detail

1O. Misreads information

Testing

Now that you have done some reading, what is the next step? You are concerned that your child is learning-disabled, or maybe a doctor or teacher has presented this possibility to you. What happens next?

First, the school usually does a bit of investigating to determine if the child's disability is caused by a poor home environment. If the child is not fed right or is abused, he or she may be negatively affected. Once it is concluded that no environmental reasons are at fault, the next direction is to make sure the child gets tested to eliminate all potential medical reasons. MRIs and EEGs are done to make sure it is not the makeup of the child's genetics and to eliminate other possibilities, such as a brain tumor.

When everything has been analyzed, the most likely reason for the struggle is the child has a legitimate learning disability. This entire process can be very hard on the parents, as you can easily feel as if the school is blaming you. But it really isn't the intended consequence. It is just a by-product of the process.

Early diagnosis, early intervention

Nowadays, we are fortunate there are many places to turn when it comes to getting a child tested for learning disabilities-even as young as a few months old. It is good to find out as soon as possible if and how your child is delayed in any way. Early testing provides a great advantage and gives more time to find the right method for the child to learn. It also gives you every opportunity to encourage the child every step of the way-from the very beginning. And encouragement is vital to your child's success.

Finding anything your child is good at is important. Make it seem as if it's the most incredible thing you have ever seen. For example, my six-year-old Mandy can set the table better than anyone else. She gets so excited to do the job. She personalizes it, too. She makes one of us have the small plate or a silly cup.

The bottom line is, she has to know she has value. She already knows that she is the slowest learner. But she also knows that she can set a table better than anyone else in the class.

School can beat kids down. John has said, "School will beat the joy out of a joyful soul." They struggle through it all day, which is why it's so important to lift their spirits at home.

Encouraging a child at every step is not the same as false praise. False praise would be telling my daughter she can write her letters better than anyone else in the class. But I do try to make true statements that praise, like "That's the best writing I've ever seen you do!"

Your child has his own needs that need to be met, and he has value as a member of your family. Make sure he knows-really understand it-by encouraging him for who he is and praising him when he has done his best.

Denial is a natural response, but instead of dwelling there, remember that God has a different plan for your child than you thought-and that's okay. More than okay, in fact.

Disability does not mean defect. It means different. Another way to put it is that your child is differently abled, not disabled.

I had a conversation once with my son Mike. He was talking about his struggle to learn to read. He said, "It's like a wall is built in front of my brain. I guess that means that I need to break the wall down. So I should be good at that since I break things all the time, right Mom?"

Find the positive, always. Read happy, positive books. Find success stories and realize they happen more often than you think. Stay near positive people and find a support group. If you can't find one, start one. You are far from alone.

Last but not least, of course-pray. Pray for your decisions. Pray for your child and those working with him or her. Pray for the friends your child spends time with. In addition, most importantly, thank God for the gift of raising your child. There is a bright spot in all of this. Be sure to find it.

Chapter 13

It's been my experience that many times you, as the parent, need to be the aggressive one with the school. I've found most schools hope you are an overprotective parent, or that your child is just a late bloomer. The school knows how hard a learning disability can be to cope with. Getting proper help and attention is hard on their budget, yet they are legally responsible for it.

And yet I believe they genuinely wish only the best for the child. So don't give up. If you do not fight for your child, no one will. You are your child's parent for a reason.

It is important to remember that it's easier to catch a fly with honey than with vinegar. Try to stay on good terms with your school. Sometimes I have taken flowers and cookies into the office. The office workers are a foundation of the school. I also give birthday gifts to the teachers and principal who go above and beyond help us. I even gave brownies to the janitors. Yes, even the janitors. Who else opens the doors after hours to get forgotten homework?

I make it a point to not give a gift to every teacher. I give gifts to those who do more. The rest of the teachers get paychecks for doing their jobs. I figure that this way the other teachers who work extra hard will know I am truly grateful for their efforts. A teacher said once, "My job is to make your job easier." She understood that my son was so stressed at school, and she wanted to do everything she could to make sure he wouldn't carry it home with him.

Proverbs 16:7 says, "When a man's ways please the Lord, he makes even his enemies be at peace with him." Not that the school is our enemy, but there can be a great tension between a parent and a school. I do my best to avoid those strains.

Taming the mother bear

I always refer to the mother bear in me who would do anything to protect my child. But it would be best for me to consider that the teachers and the school system are not trying to hurt my child. I can easily get too emotionally involved. Proverbs gives this caution: "The beginning of strife is like releasing water, therefore stop contention before a quarrel starts." (Proverbs 17:14)

One of my children had a first-year teacher. The whole school was abuzz, thrilled to have this fresh, new mind join their ranks. She had graduated from that school, and the school was very proud of that fact. She was incredibly intelligent and had scored well on state tests.

I was not so convinced that it would be a stellar year. This teacher herself had learned easily due to her intelligence therefore, she would not understand the difficulties that my child faced daily.

This teacher loved to organize. She offered 20 percent of the grade on how neat the binder was. As she stated, "It's 20 percent easy points." Right. Easy points. That's like a gymnast telling a class they can have 20 "easy points" just for doing a backflip. The entire class could train for a month, but many would never get those easy points at all.

The only requirement was keeping a binder exactly as she wanted it organized, and it guaranteed them at least partial success. But keeping a binder neat for my child was like doing a backflip. I met with this teacher after school one day to discuss why my child was failing her class. That first meeting did not go well. She explained her methods of encouraging the kids-most of which turned out to be negative reinforcements.

She made the mistake of telling me that I was being an overprotective mother who was going to ruin my kids' lives if I stayed this involved in their education. I wanted to say, "Oh, so did your four years of college give you this insight or was it your twenty-one years of being a parent?"

I was firm and took no flak from her. She really wasn't prepared to face a parent like me. College doesn't do enough to prepare teachers for involved parents. It seemed as if she viewed school as a place of comfort. Her entire life she had worked hard and made the grades she expected.

Many people go into teaching because they like school. It was a place they fit in, so why not go back? Others become teachers because they love a subject such as science or math. And some go into teaching because of the job perk of having a summer free from work.

Then there are those who simply love to teach-to work with the students. Ultimately, I feel that this particular teacher loved the students as much as she loved school. I explained how my son had scored perfectly in math on the state test the year before-but was now failing her class. I suggested that perhaps her presentation and motivation needed tweaking.

The next meeting went much better. She was so nervous at first. I pointed out, eventually, that positive reinforcement is effective for all ages and also made the point that 12-year-olds are more like children than adults. I can see why she felt that they were "little adults"-they act so maturely sometimes. It is frustrating to deal with preteens because other times they behave closer to preschoolers.

Ultimately, she was a great teacher. She had a lot of fantastic ideas. I loved her as a teacher, and after that second meeting, we got along great. I feel bad I intimidated her at first, but it turned out to be a good partnership in achieving the best education for my child.

Mother Bear Continued

The concept of the "mother bear" is something that is frequently on my mind. I was discussing this with one mother in my support group. I had asked her if she ever felt like she became a Mother Bear and was going to describe what I meant by it, but she just laughed. "You don't have to explain that," she said. She knew exactly what I meant. "That's me for more than half of my life," she said.

One of the other mothers pointed out it really can be hard to control the instinctive urge to become Mother Bear. For example, she loved her in-laws dearly and loved spending weeks visiting at their house. But one time, her father-in-law left out some sharp objects: a saw and razor blades. Her son ended up getting hold of one of these and cut up a mattress.

She had asked her father-in-law to keep these kinds of objects out of sight, but his response was that they had "never baby-proofed the house before" and that kids were just supposed to know what things not to touch.

She lost it then and really told him off. She told him her son doesn't always see the consequences of his actions until it's too late. This is the same boy who, at age five, tried to climb into the lion's den at the zoo to "pet the kitty."

This mother felt horrible about yelling at her father-in-law because he was a good grandfather. But at that moment, Mother Bear came out swinging and took over.

Advocate

I think it's a wise idea to consider getting an educational advocate. An advocate is not as emotionally involved as you are and will be objective when looking at what s best for the child without mixing in personal feelings. They also won't be swayed by budget details as school officials might be. In addition, advocates are up on all the current laws and can get the greatest amount of help for your child.

However, it's also a good idea to keep up with the laws on your own. Ask for extra testing if you are seeing results that don't seem consistent with your child's ability. Mistakes can happen, and it's up to you to make sure that your child is well taken care of. After all, no one knows your child better than you.

In one of the first IEP (Individualized Educational Program) meetings I had, I wish I had had an advocate with me. Or at least, had been more familiar with the law.

At that time, the school's largest issues were not the same concerns I had. They felt one of the doctors had misled us but I saw that the doctor's results matched my concerns. I allowed the school to make me believe that I was the ignorant one. Had I known then what I do now, the meeting would have ended differently.

At that meeting I pleaded for more help with my son's writing. I was told he didn't need it. Two years later, the same person stated that I should have asked for help

84

sooner, as it would now be a waste of time because he was so far behind.

Another unpleasant experience that could have been resolved with an advocate was when one of my sons had a misunderstanding with a teacher. It was due partially to ignorance by the teacher, but also somewhat due to a clash of personalities. The teacher gave instruction to my son, which he took literally, and it ended with the teacher calling him a liar in front of the class and being sent to detention.

I let him serve the detention but went to speak with the teacher to explain my son's reasoning. The teacher said she felt he was being blatantly disrespectful. I asked him about it, and he denied doing any of the things she accused him of.

Every other teacher had commented about how brutally honest my son is, and that he doesn't seem to have a manipulative bone in his body. He makes sure others get the bigger piece of the cake; they said. So I had a hard time believing this teacher had the full picture. She was telling me that my son was a liar and a manipulator, and I just couldn't see it.

I called a meeting but didn't take an advocate or John. The teacher ended up denying something that she had said, saying that I misunderstood her. But when I was told that my son was purposefully tossing three hours of homework, I had asked her twice to verify what she was saying before I even asked him about it. There was no misunderstanding.

In that same meeting, they also scrutinized me. They told me to open my eyes to the fact that my son was now a teenager and that teenagers lie. It happens. So they were expecting me to take the word of an adult over my son simply because of his age.

I did not and will not believe that. I trust my teens because they have earned it. Why would I not expect the most of my kids? Why would I just assume that he would lie?

I left the meeting feeling as if I had just been interrogated. My parenting skills were laid out on the table and questioned. I know that if I had an advocate or my husband with me that meeting would have ended much differently. It's hard to stand up for yourself when you're being accused, especially in such an unexpected manner.

There have been many other meetings that didn't have great results, and they have repeatedly asked me why my kids are not prepared. "Hello!" I feel like saying, "that is a symptom of ADHD."

They've asked about stained clothing (one of my kids was born with a birth defect which causes frequent bloody noses), unbrushed teeth, lateness, lost assignments or supplies, and many other things-all of which are a related to the very struggles that warrant the meeting in the first place. Instead of actively seeking to help my children, they scrutinize symptoms which are sometimes out of my control.

One time a substitute teacher who had taught my child for three days gave me parenting advice. I'm sure she meant to be helpful, but so often it is difficult not to feel offended-as if it's the fault of the parents that the children are how they are.

I understand teachers feel they know what they're talking about, and they often do, but there is a huge gap between classroom learning and life experience. This substitute teacher had no children of her own, and while I don't have a teaching degree, I've been a parent for over 20 years.

Teachers

In *Benny and Joon* (1993, MGM), Johnny Depp plays a character, Benny, who makes incredible displays of creativity. When asked if he learned his skills in school, his reply is, "No, no, I got thrown out of school for that."

The lesson here is this: teachers do not always view things with a creative eye. I feel that it's not so much a child's disability to learn as it is an inability to teach so they can understand. It's important to find what works for each individual child. If a teacher tries one method for months without good results, a change is needed.

In the teachers' defense, they often feel they are the ones left with the blame. The point is, it's no one's fault. The blame game does no one any good-not the parents, teachers, or most importantly, the students. From a parent's perspective, I feel it's very important that we learn to always address teachers with respect. I wish I could say that I have always done that, but unfortunately, I have not. There have been times I have lost my temper because I felt the teacher didn't understand the disabilities or was disrespectful to me.

One time my son's assignment was late and teacher said that he had already allowed him to hand in an overdue assignment-as if he was doing me a great favor. In reality, he was doing his job. I jumped out of the small chair I was sitting in and not-so-calmly reminded him that he just might need to put more effort into teaching my child.

"It is in the IEP that he's allowed 24 hours after I'm made aware of a missing assignment. It's your job-I don't need to thank you to do it." Unfortunately, it wasn't a stellar moment in my Christian life.

What is an IEP?

An IEP is an individual education plan that is a legal contract between you and your school. After all the testing is done, you and your spouse will meet with the head of special education, the speech therapist, social worker, homeroom teacher, and principal. Together you will go over the tests and discuss where your child is academically.

There are a few tests that are standard for most schools. Although each educator may have different preferences,

Wisc-III and Woodstock are predominantly used. It is important for you as the parent to understand the results and the scoring scale.

You are ultimately the one who will decide what needs to be done in the future. It's your responsibility to make sure that your child is receiving enough help without consuming time that isn't necessary.

The IEP will include information such as the child's age and level programming. Much of the information may be abbreviated: AE (age equivalent scores), SS (standard scores), CA (chronological age, i.e. 10.0, which means that they took the score at 10 years old). It will also contain results for the reading level, which might read as 1.5 (first year, fifth month).

Another abbreviation that you might see is RTI. RTI, or Response to Intervention, is a process designed to help the school focus on and provide high quality instruction.

Other things discussed will be behavior and ways to help deal with behaviors which aren't acceptable. There will also be a list of accommodations (examples: shortening assignments, technical assistance like laptops or calculators, etc.) that the student may have.

The RTI plan is transferable to any other school your child might attend, and while it's good to give notice to new schools, they accept the plans even from state to state.

You have the right to call a meeting if you feel there are

problems. The school needs to give you proper notice of when any meetings will be held. You do not have to sign the contract at the end of the meeting. You can take it home and reread what they decided. I look back on some meetings over the years and wish that I had waited to sign.

It is very important to understand the power of an IEP. A good place to get information is at the federal education website:

http://www.ed.gov/parents/needs/speced/iepguide/index.html

To illustrate the importance, consider the 1993 case Florence County School District Four v. Shannon Carter. The school developed an IEP for Shannon Carter that stated that she was only supposed to improve very little over the course of the year. Her parents insisted that their daughter required a more intensive program. When they were told to "take it or leave it," the family went to a private school that promised to do more.

Later, the Carters won in court and it forced the school district to reimburse the Carters for the tuition fees.

Examples from personal experience

I know from experience how difficult it can be to walk through the daily interactions and at times, miscommunications with the school.

An advocate once made this observation: "Have you ever noticed that the school always sends the teacher who's having the least amount of trouble teaching your child?" Until she said that, I had never realized it.

I've also been to meetings where the school changes a label or diagnosis. They aren't medical professionals-why do they have the authority to alter results?

It has been said Several times that my children can't learn because I haven't prepared them. One day one of my sons arrived at school with jelly all over his pants, and they said he was so embarrassed that he could not focus.

That morning right before my son got on the bus, he had toast with jelly on it. He had overloaded the bread with jelly. I removed most of the jelly. When I was not looking, he took a handful of jelly to put back on the toast and ran out the door.

After getting on the bus, he realized that he had jelly all over his hands, so he wiped them on his legs. Seeing the stains on his pants, he was so embarrassed that he covered them with his shirt, which also got his shirt messy as well.

I could not believe my eyes when he walked in the door. I understand why the school had a fit-but if they were that concerned, why didn't they call me? I work from home and could have easily brought more clothes in for him.

Looking back, I realize that he was using food as a comfort. He was stressed and ate to relieve his pain. I actually caught him hiding in a closet, shoveling food into his mouth. I have also gotten calls from the school asking me if I ever brushed my kindergartener's teeth.

My daughter had told them, "Mom doesn't use toothpaste." It was true. For two years, I didn't use toothpaste in her mouth because she was sensitive about tastes and textures. The dentist needed two people to hold her down just to look at her teeth for a check-up. Our dentist told me to just brush her teeth without toothpaste for a while. I told her teacher this and said I would send a doctor's note to verify the reasons. They said it wasn't necessary and not to bother.

My thought? If it's not worth a document, it doesn't warrant a phone call. They seemed to just be letting me know they were watching me. I hoped that they made the call out of loving concern for my daughter's well-being.

When the school tested Mike's reading, I received one phone call a day giving me different reasons why his scores were low. The first was to inform me he had worn his dad's glasses and not his own. (Mike didn't want to wear glasses, so John got a matching pair-in hindsight, not something I would recommend.) I took his glasses to the school, but the teachers felt he was so embarrassed that he could not learn.

The second call was to tell me that Mike said he didn't eat much for breakfast. "Not much" for Mike was a bowl of cereal and a banana. He loves to eat. Both phone calls were to inform me of problems that originated in the home. I told John I was afraid that they would blame my parenting for the poor results on his reading test, and I was right.

The third call was to ask me if Mike got to bed on time because he seemed tired while he was taking the reading test. Of course he was tired-it was the third day of a very stressful test.

Chapter 14

My friend Krissy comments I make friends everywhere I go, and yet I have had several confrontations with teachers. I'm not someone who likes conflict, and it's hard to explain to people who haven't had to fight for the basics needed to educate their children, but I will do what I need to do to help my kids.

One of my sons had a conflict with a teacher, and I believe it was a simple misunderstanding of my son's thought process. The whole mess started with a pencil. My kids have a hard time remembering pencils. So to alleviate the problem, I bought pencils in bulk and leaving them in their classrooms. I figured it was fair as long as every student had the same opportunity to take from the box.

But I had many teachers argue that I was not teaching life skills, like having to learn to be prepared on their own. I didn't really think it was more important than passing the class and learning the subject. Anyway, my son came home with a detention because he had "stolen a pencil," but when I talked to him about it, he said he took it from the pencil box.

I had many talks with the teacher about the incident, but she flat out stated that she thought my son was a liar and was manipulating me. It's a fact I find hard to believe when I hear from so many other teachers and people who know he is honest, warm-hearted, and unselfish.

What should I think when a teacher telling me that the same child is lying and manipulating? It didn't make sense. She also told me he was taking completed homework out of his bag and throwing it in the garbage. We worked for three hours on that homework-why would he do that? That was my final straw.

God knows our frustrations and sees our difficulties. And despite the misunderstandings, God called us to love everyone-even and especially the teachers who sometimes view us as an obstacle.

I love my children, and I want the best for them, but I also love each teacher. I'm not perfect, but I do my best to strive to handle each situation in a way that glorifies God.

I have had some wonderful relationships with teachers and school officials. It amazes me sometimes when I speak to parents who don't even know their principal. By the end of the school year, I usually know the phone extension of almost everyone in the school.

I have taken the special education classes required to get a teaching certificate. They don't really deal with the common situations that occur working with learning-disabled students and their parents. Communication, which is vital to the success of all involved, does not come easily and should be more of a focus of the training in my opinion.

Chapter 15

It's easy to feel inadequate as a parent when you socialize with other parents. You will hear them talk about their child who has an all-A report card or was invited to yet another birthday party.

Of course there's nothing wrong with being proud of your child. But it can be frustrating knowing you studied for two hours with your child so he could get a "C" on that spelling test, while the bragging parent read over the words once or twice with her child, if that.

So many times I have felt that other parents or people have been rude while showing their ignorance of learning disabilities. They asked one parent I know not to take her child to the grocery store anymore until she could learn to control him. That mother replied "Oh, wow-I didn't know your store offered free delivery. Thanks."

The point is dealing with learning disabilities isn't the most comfortable or socially acceptable thing in the minds of the majority, but we as parents have to do the best we can. Our kids aren't perfect, and neither are we.

Another parent of an autistic son was asked sympathetically, "Do you know if he will ever be able to work or get married?" The parent said, "No, we don't know yet. By the way, I'm sorry to hear your engineering son lost his job and isn't able to work-and I'm also sorry to hear about your daughter's divorce." Maybe the comment wasn't the godliest, but it reveals something: even without disabilities, children have difficulties in life.

One mother from my support group told a story about the frustration of just trying to pull off the simple task of going shopping with friends. It would literally take her two hours to get out the door.

Once at the mall, she would end up pushing a screaming child around, pausing many times for tries to make her son happy. She had fed him, changed him, and held him as her friend's child smiled contentedly from his stroller. When she called it quits, she didn't even get out of the mall before a total stranger said, "Why don't you feed that baby or something?"

As you might imagine, it devastated her. Why couldn't she do what others seem to take for granted in a normal day?

Daily life can be hard, and a lot of times my first reaction is not a holy one. But all I can do is pray to see others through the Lord's eyes, to love them as he does.

It's not that I want anyone to pity me or my children. I love my kids the way they are-absolutely. Sometimes I wish that people could be a little more understanding, to see life through different eyes.

People who don't live in your world are not going to understand that this affects your whole life. One mom was telling me how she has to plan every little thing for her son who is OCD and ADHD. Her son hates the summer because there is too much freedom-he doesn't want to be told to "just go play" because it is too open-ended.

He can't handle being over-stimulated, so they even have to be careful which campgrounds they go to. They can't just make a quick run to the store when they've run out of toilet paper. She knows, because she tried it once. Her son had an anxiety attack, and halfway through the shopping trip he ended up sitting on the floor, rocking back and forth. People just stopped and stared at him. Could anyone have even thought to say, "Can I help you in any way?"

The same mom also said her son loves baseball, so they thought it might be a good idea to try attending a White Sox game because he could easily handle local baseball games.

The experience turned out to be entirely too much. And so it goes that every experience becomes a learning one. Now her son is a little older, and he can express when something is too much for him.

When he was little, he didn't know how to communicate that fact, and he would get so upset and could not talk or even communicate simple facts, like being hungry. She had to learn to read the signs of his behavior until he had matured enough to speak his own thoughts. Things like that are a reality, and yes, they put a damper on the social life for that time.

Another couple whom I've talked to have an autistic child. They felt like prisoners in their own home. The husband had been in the military and had been specially trained on how to deal with being in captivity. Those same tactics came in handy in functioning day-to-day during that time period.

Since their son did not handle change well, they had to forego most social invitations and stayed home. They had a large family and just to keep up with the laundry, grocery shopping, and doctor visits. They chose their son's needs above their "house-keeper of the year" award, if there were such a thing.

But that concept can sometimes be hard for other people to grasp. They grew tired of having couples come over because they often ended up receiving advice about how they could keep a cleaner house. It got to where they stopped having others come visit so they wouldn't have to deal with the critiques of their ignorant peers.

Some misguided advice was to make new friends within the world of the disabled, because in the "real world," parents would never understand. People also tried to offer help in ways they thought were good, weren't actually beneficial.

Yet another couple saw changes in their social life, but viewed it more positively. "It didn't stop our socializing, It changed it. And I would never have met all the wonderful people involved with the Special Olympics if our life had not changed."

Chapter 16

John and I have friends whose children do well in school with little help. When they heard that one of my sons would attend a school for kids with special needs, they said, "Well, at least he is only disabled in the classroom." Oh, how wrong they were. Learning disabilities will influence every area of life. It is easy to feel inadequate as a parent. Your child will probably have a hard time doing simple things like getting dressed. It could be a major struggle to make sure that your kids leave the house with their pants and a shirt on in the right direction.

One of the tough things for me personally is the judgment of my own family. I am not alone in this; many people in my support group have experienced rejection from the family in one form or another. Some grandparents have even invited certain siblings over because the other is "too hard" or embarrassing in front of their friends.

It's hard to explain the pain you feel when your own family rejects you. It rips a hole in your heart. And it might become necessary to withdraw from the presence of certain family members if it affects your child's self-worth.

I was discussing this concept of family misunderstanding with someone. My friend said, "Okay, I know I am not Mrs. Cleaver, but why did God make my sister perfect so that my mom has a close comparison ready at hand to critique my mothering skills?"

That seems to be true so often. I seem to hear the words "We are concerned" a lot from those who judge my children. To me, being concerned is a feeling, not an action. Caring is an action. Caring would be stopping by my house to say hi. Taking the kids out for an afternoon of fun. Seeing them a few times a year to get to know the ways they are gifted.

But those who seem so often "concerned" usually sit on the sidelines, far from the action of life, yet so certain of everything we're doing wrong. I realize that this could make me sound bitter. And admittedly, it takes a lot of Scriptural gargling to wash out the bitter after-effects of pure ignorance.

Other parents will also offer pointless and impractical advice because they see a symptom but don't understand the underlying reasons. Suggesting that a child who struggles to remember things be given a checklist might seem logical, but in this reality, you've just given your overwhelmed child one more thing to remember.

After I told a story about a typical chaotic morning, a mom said, "Oh, well I know what you're doing wrong." As if she had suddenly solved every one of my life problems.

"You should not be waking your kids up. I never get mine up. They have alarm clocks for a reason," she said. "I also never take them a lunch if they forgot it. Trust me. Your children will remember next time." An alarm clock?

Oh, what is that? I wanted to say. Therefore, if my children use alarm clocks, their disabilities will just go away?

If letting my kids stay at school without a lunch or their forgotten assignment just once could help cure the learning disabilities that would be great. Perhaps if we let them fall flat on their faces a few times that will prove more effective than adapting teaching methods to their learning styles?

As a side note, I had been telling a story-not asking for advice. This mom was so willing to point out all the things I did wrong. I know she had good intentions, but it still hurt. I should have told her the story of a morning in my house when the boys had to show me a snake which they found, or the day our dog chased a groundhog in our basement. Can you imagine the advice she would have given me then?

It's important to keep in mind that kids with learning disabilities strain themselves getting ready for school enough as it is. They feel inadequate when compared to other students. Letting them go hungry would only make them a target once more, and unnecessarily so. Proverbs 10:13 says, "Wisdom is found on the lips of him who has understanding." It is hard to deal with the ignorance of others.

A friend once made a comment informing me that not all learning-disabled children are "slow"-some have high IQ's. She meant it as a compliment, but it didn't land that way. I wanted to say that, yes, I was quite aware that my

102

son wasn't "slow."

Other times people will say, "He can't be in special ed. He looks normal." What does "normal" look like? Learning disabilities don't have a "look" any more than Americans have a "look." An American can be black, white, Indian, and so on. So can a learning-disabled child.

I will admit that the life skills of brushing their hair or putting clothes on in the right direction are often a struggle. Just getting to school with the homework you spent three hours on the night before can prove difficult. So parents need to choose their battles. Schoolwork comes first.

I'm not saying that every child who struggles in learning has messy hair or disheveled clothing. The bias of saying that all kids with learning disabilities look one way or another is just as ridiculous as saying that all children without learning disabilities look the same as well.

I understand that other mothers are only trying to help. But each family has to find out what works for them. Just remember to let the advice of inexperienced family and friends roll off your back. Try to remember that God has given you this challenge because He has a higher purpose. Your child wasn't given to you by accident. So trust He will give you wisdom to walk through it.

My friend Kathy has five children and two are handicapped. She has felt a lot of judgment and has felt hurt at times. She went to church with a family who didn't interact with her, even though they sat in the same church for many years.

This other family ended up with a handicapped grandchild. That grandmother asked Kathy questions on a weekly basis, like "What does it feel like?" or "What did you have to go through?" Understandably so, it was a little difficult for Kathy to process the sudden interest in her perspective after being invisible for so long. The grandmother had the right motive-she wanted to help her grandchild-but it hurt Kathy to know that the woman had never cared before.

Chapter 17

My son may look as if there should be no problem for him to learn, and many times others will become frustrated while trying to work with him. They will feel that he is acting slow or ignoring social signs and just being rude. I firmly believe ADHD is not an excuse for bad behavior. But what others might view as "rudeness" might simply be unintentional ignorance on my son's part.

My friend Nina has two daughters with Down Syndrome. She will have people treat her girls like babies because of how they look. A good policy for everyone to adopt would be to get to know a child before assuming the worst. Don't judge a child by the way that they look. Likewise, don't assume that because they "look normal" that they can meet your standards.

One mom I talked to told me she had found a way to help people understand the developmental delay of her son. She could say that he was delayed, or she could say that he was autistic, but either way, people did not get it. Instead, she started to say that her son was a Special Olympics athlete, and then the light bulb would go on in other people's heads.

Sometimes people just need a more "visual" example to understand what autism is. It doesn't mean having a child who is "Rain Man" or a kid who spins a plate on the floor. At the Special Olympics you will see all different looks and actions-no two participants are the same. But for some reason, associating her child with the

Special Olympics really made it click with people who otherwise couldn't understand.

The compassion of fellow Christians

I have talked to enough different parents to make me believe ignorance about the needs of Special Ed kids is pretty much across the board-Christians and non-Christians alike. I guess I had just been hoping to find that Christians would be more compassionate, similar to how people assume that children attending a Christian school will act more like Christians than believers who attend public schools.

It's not the kids that make the school Christian, but rather the curriculum that they teach. In the same way, people who attend church aren't necessarily any more compassionate than the next person. But I keep hoping and wishing for that to be the case.

As a Christian, one of the hardest things for me to handle is the uncompassionate brothers and sisters in the church. Many believers have the attitude that if we prayed about ADHD or a learning disability, they would go away.

My sister's husband has an amputated leg. No Christian has said, "If you prayed with real faith, then God will grow the leg back." We all know that God can do anything. This same sister has a daughter who deals with migraines and depression. Many people think God could heal her if her faith were stronger. Where do we come off judging the level of someone else's faith?

Others feel it's an issue of "sparing the rod and spoiling the child" (Proverbs 13:24). Either way, it is hard for some people to understand that others have a different path than they do.

Many times, there is a struggle involved, but the suffering is not a punishment from God. The book of Job is a prime example of this. James 1 says to "consider it pure joy" when facing trials, because they produce perseverance. Perseverance, in turn, brings about maturity and faith so that the believer is equipped for every situation. (James 1:2-4, 12)

I have heard from more than one Christian professional Drs. Dobson and Lemen, for example, who both believe ADHD is no excuse for bad behavior. I agree with that statement and admire both men. But the advice doesn't help when you're trying to figure out the line between bad behavior done out of selfish impulses or whether it stems from the fact that the child is completely ignorant of what's going on around them.

On top of that, what if the bad behavior stems from the anxiety that the child is experiencing? These kids' lives are not without stress. Some react outwardly to release the stress.

Poor social skills will also present as bad behavior. A parent of an ADHD child needs to discern twenty-four hours a day what the motivation is behind her child's behavior, and the best way of responding to it. This is no small task and a tiring job.

I have friends who were asked not to bring their child to church because he couldn't sit still. This mother said, "Christians are the first to say I will pray for you. That is their out. But non-Christians tend to be the ones who actually reach out and help, or just simply stop by for a cup of coffee to catch up while the Christians are at their Bible studies, praying for me." It's a realization that stings, but can be so true.

Talking to another mother about the reactions she gets from other Christians, she said, "Well, in general Christians and non-Christians are both ignorant." I asked her if she had ever read the book *The New Strong-Willed Child* (Dr. James Dobson, Tyndale House Publishers, 2004), and she surprised me when she said, "Well, I have six copies of the book, each one given by loving members of my church. All who told me the book would change my life."

She attended a church with a lot of families that home school. They would tell her that the answer to her family issues was to home school. There's nothing wrong with homeschooling, but it's not the best for every child's life. Her son was OCD, so if her other children who she did home-school were sick, they would go to the doctor and do math in the waiting room. But this wasn't an option for her son because he didn't know how to process the change.

Dr. Dobson's books have great advice, but they will not get rid of disabilities. Church members might have been more helpful just offering to do simple tasks, like running to the store so she could keep things consistent with her son. Instead of tossing books at her, which added

108

one more thing into her busy, overwhelmed life.

Another mother had a child with POO and sensory integration problems. Her child wanted to join the church and they had to wear robes during the ceremony. There was no way that her son could handle wearing the material that they made the robe from.

So they bought a nice shirt and tie, and he looked so nice and was so excited about being able to officially join the church. But many members of the congregation wrote formal letters of complaint about the robe-less child. Shouldn't the focus have been on the fact that he was joining the church?

A dad told me the only thing that really bothers him is the huge response and involvement that worldwide missions get, yet his family is ignored and asked to quiet down at church. He feels the church has a mission field practically on their doorstep, and they're completely blind to it.

It's hard to endure these sorts of comments and situations with a positive attitude, but instead of getting frustrated, we need to help educate those who are ignorant. If the misplaced comments of other parents can hurt me how much more so will the uninformed remarks of their peers will hurt my kids?

It's important to give support to those around you, but also to get advice from others who have walked the path before you. Talk to other parents who have faced these difficulties. Even if the specifics aren't the same, it can uplift and be enlightening to hear from others who haven't had a conventional route.

Chapter 18

I've had experiences with other parents who try to point out that their children are getting a great education at the same school where my child is struggling-from the same teachers who I feel aren't doing their jobs.

The key difference is that the other parents' children don't require many IEP meetings if any at all. These parents question why I get so involved. Don't I trust the school? When you become a parent who speaks up to get help for your children, people will feel that you are bashing the school itself. Because many people pride themselves on the schools that their children attend-sometimes even moving to a specific area just so their kids can go to a specific school-they take perceived insults against the school quite personally.

They don't comprehend that even in the best school districts, it is almost impossible for each child to get exactly what he needs, especially when the child needs more than the average student. Sometimes the only thing that can one can do is to pray for the friends, neighbors, and school workers-pray that they understand and can gain a different perspective.

Also, it's wise to realize that although people may speak differently about you and your family, it's pointless to get angry. Proverbs speaks often about proper answers and responses (Proverbs 15:23, 29). I have experienced slander from various people who just didn't understand me or my kids. It hurts terribly, hearing untrue things that have been assumed and repeated about your family, but anger is not the way to handle the pain.

Dealing with other parents or family members who are ignorant about what you're dealing with is frustrating. But it's possible to handle that frustration instead of getting angry. Consider asking them to read up on learning disabilities. Suggest that they watch some DVDs dealing with the specific difficulties your family is facing. There are many good options out there, and most are easily obtained from the library. My favorite DVD is *How Difficult Can It Be?* by Dr. Rick Lavoie.

Chapter 19

Real Advice: Pre-School

- Play lots of games and let them win. It builds self-esteem. Make shapes and letters out of everything. (Examples: bread, cheese, clay, play dough-the messier, the better. Make learning fun!) Bill Vaughn once said, "A three-year-old is a being who gets almost as much fun out of a fifty-six-dollar swing set as it does out of finding a small, green worm." (You need not spend a lot of money on supplies!)

- Draw letters and shapes in sand or flour.

- Draw letters and shapes with a squirt gun on the sidewalk.

- Practice writing their name with glue and glitter.

- Explain any new situation and prepare them for it. (Example: tell your child they may touch nothing in the store-don't wait till they have already tried to pick everything up.) Be direct with any instructions. (Example: Don't climb on that tree or any other trees in the park.)

- Establish eye contact with them to make sure they are paying attention, but remember that inability to hold eye contact can be part of some disabilities, so don't get upset or yell if they are easily distracted.

- Have your child repeat instructions back to you.

- Give one-step instructions until you can build up to two-step tasks.

- Picture books provide great opportunities to help children learn consequences by seeing what happens next in a story.

- Being read to helps a child expand their vocabulary. Make up stories during periods of waiting (in waiting rooms, car rides, etc.) to build imagination.

- Give the kids wiggle room and don't expect them to sit perfectly still.

- Be firm when necessary, but do not yell.

- Try to be consistent with a schedule but don't freak out when life hits. Be flexible.

- Play fun games like "button, button, who's got the button?"

- Make working on large motor skills fun. (Example: Monkey bars and balance beams.)

- Reinforce their worth as children of God, and that they are gifted, just like anyone else.

- Pray with them.

- Visually track progress with them, don't just tell them what to do. They need to learn to think about what they are doing, not just get used to you telling them what to do. (Example: Use Popsicle sticks in a jar to represent tasks that need to be completed, and then move them to another jar to represent tasks that are done.)

- Make personal hygiene fun. (Example: When my daughter shows me her clean teeth, I act like they are so clean and bright that I am blinded.)

- Try to understand physical sensitivities. (Example: If a child is sensitive to certain textures in their mouth, it can often be as painful as sandpaper.)

- Potty training has to be done in their time frame- you cannot force it. Don't make accidents a big ordeal. Be patient with them.

Real advice: Kindergarten-3rd grade

- Make letters and shapes fun. (Example: Put pancake batter into a squeeze bottle and make letter-shaped pancakes or write words on thick rubber bands so that when you stretch the bands, the letters pull apart. Make letters out of sandpaper or carpet so that the kids can feel the letters and see if the letter is facing the right direction.)

- Explain new situations. (Example: When going on a field trip, make sure your child knows the rules haven't changed from what they follow at school or that church is a place where they need to be quiet.)

- Be aware of other children who do not understand the differences between them and your child.

- Read to and with them. (Example: a chapter a night before bed.)

- Don't overwhelm them with too many options, but still give them a choice. (Example:

- Two snack options and have them choose one or the other. Don't ask an open-ended question, like "What do you want for a snack?")

- Understand any sensitivity they may have. (Example: clothing textures, tastes, etc.)

- Allow them to have their own style, but train them so they can make wise decisions.

- Explain that their body is God's temple, and it's respectful to clothe it appropriately. (Example: Explain that if they wear snow boots and shorts to church, others might make fun.)

- Make it a practice to set clothes out the night before-that way there are no last-minute decisions.

- Make sure they understand that movies are not real.

- Discuss human nuances, like facial expressions and tone of voice, so that they get better at reading what's going on around them.

- Practice writing in creative ways. (Example: use colorful markers or write with cake frosting.)

- Make sure your child knows their last name and how to spell and write it.

- Think ahead and anticipate what might go through your child's head. Know your child so you can prepare them for every situation. (Example: If I was Billy, and I was at the zoo, would I want to climb the walls, etc.?)

- Daily remind them of their gifts and let them know God's love for them won't ever end and pray with them and for them.

- Use timers to help them understand and comprehend time frames. (Example: So they can get a feel for how long ten minutes really is.)

- Buy clothes that make getting dressed easier. (Example: Velcro shoes instead of shoelaces and elastic waist pants instead of buttons and zippers.)

- Label clothing to help them get dressed properly. (Example: "B" for back and "F" for front or draw a face on their shoes so that one half is on the right and one half on the left.)

- Help your child to succeed by not setting them up for failure. (Example: Don't give them a task you know they will struggle with.)

- Find creative ways to make it easier for them to talk about their feelings. (Example: use puppets.)

- Know of their limitations and make others aware who might unknowingly put them in an embarrassing situation. (Example: Make sure the Sunday school teacher knows they aren't able to read aloud.)

- If your child has to be on medication, make sure they know the meds just enhance who they are and that it isn't the medicine itself that makes them better or smarter.

- Encourage their creative side. (Example: Let them draw a series of pictures while you write the words so they have made a book or help them design and create their own pop-up books.)

- Make things as visual as possible.

- Reward them for not giving up.

- Do not compare them to their siblings, and do not reward for "A" grades, but rather for doing their best.

- Point out examples of others who have overcome learning challenges.

- Play counting and sorting games. (Example: Count blue cars or big trucks while driving or count train cars while waiting for a train. Have them cut out pictures of cats and dogs from magazines and help them make a collage by sorting and gluing the pictures.)

Real advice: 4th-8th grades

- Know that peer pressure is increasing dramatically.

- Give them counsel with choosing friends. (Example: "Wow, that child didn't treat you very well-maybe you should ask another friend to go to the movies?")

- Be aware that life is getting harder as they compare themselves to those around them. The comparison is inevitable.

- Be sensitive to their feelings.

- Help them stay organized by giving them a daily planner. Fill out the initial information, but slowly hand over the writing and planning to them.

- Try to analyze and be aware of how and why you're helping your child, and find a proper balance. Helping too much or not enough can have detrimental effects on your child.

- Don't allow your child to get overloaded. If things are too much, figure out what can be minimized or eliminated.

- Teach them tools of organization. (Example: Color-coded binders and folders are helpful for organizing school information.)

- Communicate with your child's teachers at the start of the school year and make sure they have read up on your child's IEP so they know your child's strengths and weaknesses.

- Continue to know of clothing choices and manner of dress. (Example: It may still be a weakness to put a shirt on backward.)

- Choose your battles.

- Get to know your janitors so that when a book is forgotten, you can still get in after hours.

- Diet is very important. Make sure they are getting balanced meals, and if they are on a restricted diet, make sure that the appropriate authorities are aware.

- Set a routine sleep schedule.

- Realize that there are attention span limitations. (Example: If you are spending two hours every night on homework, make sure your teachers know this and that it isn't possible to do anymore.)

- Make sure when your child is punished that they understand why and talk about what else could have been done in the particular situation.

- Reinforce the positive. (Example: If they missed 25 questions, focus on how many they got right.)

- Be prepared for inconsistencies and don't let them ruffle you.

- Understand there will be bad days and accept that. Celebrate the good days, but don't try to hide from the bad.

- Keep up with new technology. (Example: There are pens that can actually read books on CD, and computer programs which can all make your child's studying easier.)

- Calculators are great tools.

- Get creative with organization. (Example: Use clear plastic bags for classes which require a lot of things, that way they can run down a checklist without having to remove anything and won't risk losing it in the process.)

- Use zippered binders for organization. (Example: Papers can fall out of plain folders, but if it is zipped in, there's less chance of that.)

- Encourage creativity. (Example: Have your kids make up stories and tell them to you.)

- Be specific in questions that you ask.

- Make reading fun. (Example: Read cereal boxes each morning.)

- Remember your child is going to be more immature than others his or her age. Do not expect them to start acting their age just because they have advanced grades.

- Don't force socialization. Let them move into it in their own timing.

- Learning-disabled kids can often take statements very literally. Be aware of that.

- Graph paper is a great tool to help practice writing.

- Don't compare one day to the next. There will be good days and bad days. (Example: Saying things like, "I know you can do this-you did it yesterday!")

- Get a dictionary for poor spellers. It allows them to look words up as they hear them in their head.

Real advice: High school and adulthood

- At this age, your children do not really want their parents to love them so openly, so leave Bible verses highlighted in their lunch sacks or on their bed. This affirms that God loves them, and so do you, without being intrusive.

- Buy a copy machine. It's easy to lose things, but some with learning disabilities have more trouble that weakness. Avoid unnecessarily lost papers by making multiple copies. (Example: Copy completed homework so when the math paper you worked on for 2 hours is nowhere to be found, your child turns in the completed copy.)

- Peer pressure is incredibly difficult at this point. Know of those factors. (Example: Sometimes a teen's only goal is to make it through the day without being humiliated.)

- Get involved in their lives. (Example: Have pizza parties so they can invite friends over.)

- Know their friends and have conversations with them. This will help you be aware if they are spending time with people who are treating them with respect. (Example: It is harder now than ever with texting, cell phones, and the internet, but it is very important to know your child is hanging out with spiritually grounded kids.)

- Communicate with your child and make sure they understand rules, limitations, and the reasons behind them. (Example: Make sure they know a curfew is not about a lack of trust but is motivated by love and protection.)

- When they get ready to apply for a job, have them pick up applications and bring them home. That way, if there is a question you are there to help them answer it correctly.

- Teach them how common things work in the adult world. Training kids in life skills doesn't stop once they can dress themselves. (Example: Gas pumps and other things that most might take for granted. If they missed a bill payment, discuss with them what they might have spent the late fee money on so they are more inclined to remember next time.)

- Remind them of common courtesy. (Example: When and how to interrupt another adult.) Teach them how to respectfully be their own advocate.

- Make them aware of disability laws especially any that might pertain to them.

- Know when they are using their disability as an excuse and call them on it.

- Try to be understanding and aware of self-esteem issues. It's not something that necessarily gets better as they grow up. (Example: I have been driving to the same doctor for years and on my 19th visit, I got lost. It's so embarrassing.)

- Make sure that your child's teachers keep your child's information confidential. (Example: If they allow your child extra time to complete an assignment, have the teacher collect it a time when others are not around.)

- Praise them when they accomplish and succeed at basic life skills.

- Remember that they don't have to organize like everyone else as long as they find a method that works. (Example: If they can find their keys and assignments, even if it's not where you would keep them, let them be.)

- Don't put them on the spot. (Example: Having them read out loud in front of a group if they weren't expecting to.)

- Communication with young adults is not always easy, but don't let that discourage you.

- Find time to talk with them. A car is always a good place.

- If your child doesn't want to work with you, find a trusted Christian mentor who they can confide in.

- Make your main goal as a parent to let your children develop their own relationships with Christ.

Important note to remember

Learning-disabled children are not slow, lazy, or uncaring, even though it's a common misconception. They may need extra support, training, and reassurance to succeed in life, but that doesn't make them any less gifted or valuable. Make sure that you continually remind them of this and make them aware of their great worth.

Chapter 20

I started a support group at my church. We help each other out and try to have speakers come to give us advice. If possible, find a support group near you and make a commitment to go. Take a friend or family member with you for added support. I'm not in it for pity or a lot of help-it's just nice and refreshing to be around people who really understand what you're going through on many levels.

Starting the support group really helped me. I also received great advice from the senior pastor, Pastor Jim, at my church. He has dealt with disabilities and could speak from the experience and wisdom of many years. Pastor Jim said, "There are people who you'll need to inform by opening your mouth. On the other hand, there are others who will be better informed by you shutting your mouth and praying." Sometimes we need to allow God to do the moving. I have trouble with the part about being quiet, but it's good for me to learn to truly rely on Him.

Awareness

As the kids get older, they are self-conscious and aware of the fact that they are learning-disabled. It's important to be sensitive to their feelings. We as parents need to help them to not be ashamed, but to become advocates for themselves. It's a tightrope to walk, teaching them to be aggressive, but not disrespectful.

Also, it's vital to instill in them a greater perspective than their own-especially that of the Lord's. Train them to be thankful for the way they were made, weaknesses and all. God uses our weaknesses for His glory, so there's no reason to be ashamed of our lack of perfection.

Learning-disabled children have a high rate of dropping out of school. Suicide and depression rates are higher as well. They also have higher rates of residence in juvenile homes, eating disorders, drug, and alcohol addiction. They deal with more rejection and pain than the average student, and so are more prone to being pulled into the darker areas of life. Learning-disabled children need fan clubs. We, as parents, need to affirm them daily.

To illustrate the stark reality they face, consider some following potential characteristics of learning-disabled people:

Low self-esteem

- Poor school performance because of difficulty in writing, reading, or mathematics
- Depression
- Succumbing to peer pressure
- Coordination difficulties
- Contrast that with the following characteristics of those who struggle with substance abuse:
- Low self-esteem

- Academic struggles or failure
- Loneliness or depression
- Succumbing to peer pressure

The similarities are scary. God loves us unconditionally. We need to do the same, to the best of our abilities. We are daughters and sons of the King-yet how many princes and princesses walk around feeling bad about themselves because they don't know their true worth? 1 Peter speaks of us as a chosen generation and God's own special people. (1 Peter 2:9) Proverbs 14:26 says, "In the fear of the Lord there is strong confidence, and His children will have a place of refuge."

What can we learn from these verses? God loves us, values us, and prepares for us a place of safety and care. As parents, part of our job is to do the same for our children; to be a haven from the rest of the world.

Chapter 21

"Most of the things worth doing in the world had been declared impossible before they were done." Louis D'Brandies. Just because they diagnose your child with a learning disability, it doesn't mean his future is dim. It will be difficult and trying, but it can lead to developing him into a stronger person. It can bring out unexpected creativity because he'll be more inclined to be creative.

The old saying, "Great minds think alike" is not entirely true. New ideas which change the world are just that- new. They are not the same old, same old. Encourage his own unique perspective.

I saw a cartoon once about a group of penguins and a peacock. All the penguins move alike and look the same. They are quiet and like to be in unison.

Then there is this peacock. He looks different and walks his own way, proud to be what he is. Wouldn't it be a shame to miss the beauty of the peacock because we were too preoccupied with doing things the penguin way?

That's how we need to encourage our kids. They will recognize they're different, but don't miss the opportunity to show them that different can be an advantage. One of my sons was helping the adult Sunday school pack cookies for the homeless. They were boxing them and putting stickers on the outside. After a while, we ran out of stickers.

Most of the adults were content to quit and go have coffee. But my son who was 10 wanted to improvise by taking markers to label the boxes. He was thinking out of the box, driven by love and compassion. I made sure I bragged about that situation to others when I knew he could hear me. He wasn't a kid who appreciated public displays of affection, but I knew those positive words would mean the world to him.

I read a quote in the Wall Street Journal some time ago, from the mother of the inventor of the electronic airplane ticket. She would tell her son to look at his hand-all the fingers are different for a reason. If they were the same, the hand wouldn't function properly. Yet she felt that the school wanted all the children to conform to the same pattern. Her son just never fit that mold.

Society itself seems to want everyone to stay within the confines of the usual, the expected, that "Be Like Mike" mentality. But that isn't really how we're made to be.

Another good analogy is this: six clear, glass vases are on a shelf. All of them are very similar. If someone added a bright blue vase, it might look odd, out of place, like it shouldn't be there. But take the same vase and put it in the middle of a table. Add flowers to it and it has become a lovely centerpiece and conversation starter. It catches the light and brightens the room.

You need to find the spot where your child can be used by God to brighten up a room. Make him proud of who he is. He is, after all, God's child-what could be more infinitely valuable than that?

God's plan

One reason we as parents can feel our children's lives are bleak is that we miss the big picture. What is God's plan for success? What is success? Is it a degree, or a powerful position?

Material things don't matter to God, and neither does the world's definition of success. So what are we worrying about, really? What God requires of us is to love justice, mercy, and to walk humbly. (Jeremiah 6:8) You can do all that the Lord requires of you without achieving the pinnacle of the world's success.

I understand the feeling of worrying about your children. Kids need to understand life and at the least need to learn enough to provide for themselves. Learning to count change, for example, is vital so they aren't taken advantage of. Starting to be self-sufficient enough to survive and provide for themselves may be a long road, but we need to remember that all things are possible through Jesus.

To help prepare your child for the future, we as parents need to educate ourselves in all the methods available to help them learn. There are many therapy options out there-it's just a matter of finding the right one. Identify what is holding your child back. For example, maybe he is struggling to read. Why? The school says he is learning-disabled. What does that mean? Does he need eye therapy? Can his eyes focus together? Can he hear, not just sounds, but the phonic differences in sounds? There are countless avenues to look at.

130

The reading world is full of experts who feel that their method is the best. To me it's simple. Work with one, and if your child finds success, then that's great. If not, move on to something else. There are endless options, so don't be discouraged when one doesn't work out.

Ultimately, it's up to you to discover what clicks with your child. Schools are usually sold on one particular method, especially because it costs money to be trained in multiple teaching avenues. They purchase curriculum to back up their particular method, so they will not be thrilled at your insistence to try something else. It isn't that they don't care; from a basic standpoint, they are running a business and need to keep expenses down.

There are many successful people in the world who also have disabilities. The owner of Kinko's could barely read and yet started and continues to run a successful business. Henry Winkler, a successful actor, is dyslexic. Charles Schwab is learning-disabled. Tom Cruise is also dyslexic. Michael Naranjo, a famous sculptor, is blind.

Notice the word "is". Yes, it's true; you don't outgrow these disabilities. But you can educate your child differently and teach him to cope and adapt. For example, I still have trouble distinguishing right from left. To help with that, I wear a ring on my left hand. As a child, I wore a watch on the left.

From all the reading that I have done, the one thing that successful disabled people have in common was support from those who loved them: moms and dads to cheer them on, positive spouses and friends to encourage them along the way.

I'm sure you've heard the old story about the two children, one a pessimist and one an optimist. The father put the optimist in a room full of horse poop and the pessimist in a room full of brand-new toys. He left them there for an hour.

At the end of the hour, the pessimist child was crying because he was afraid he would break the toys, but the optimist was laughing and jumping up and down in the poop-filled room. It flabbergasted the father. "Why are you happy?" he asked. The son replied: "With this much poop, there has to be a pony in here somewhere!"

I love this story. Life is what you make of it. So help your son or daughter find their "pony." We always talk about our gifts from God. Some gifts are easier to see than others, but every child is special in his or her own way. One of my sons has a heart of gold. We have always stressed this gift to him.

Look at how your children react to different situations. What do they do when they think that no one is looking? Can they sing, or do they have any other special talents? Trust me, it won't be as hard as you think to find a pony, no matter how much poop seems to be in the room. Remember, this is your child, and you know them better than anyone else. Help them find their pony and let them know it.

Chapter 22

Making sure you have the right diagnosis is critical. Outside testing is a good option since it will remove any chance of bias that the school might have. It's also vital to find a doctor you can trust. Be attentive to who you choose. Some seem to offer up generic diagnoses for every child that walks through the door. You need someone who is caring and genuinely invested in finding the right answers for his patients.

As an example, I have been to doctors who began writing out prescriptions before I had even finished trying to explain my concerns about the child's behavior. To me, that is not a good sign of a caring doctor. Look for a physician who takes the time to understand your child and their behavior.

If you are dealing with the possibility of an ADD or ADHD child, make doubly sure you trust your doctor. Medication should never be prescribed or accepted lightly!

Not every child does great on medication either. It is a frustrating choice for a parent to make, I am well aware. Not only do you have to worry about the side effects, but now you enter a whole new arena of opinions and arguments. There are the natural vs. medication debates, and in that realm, many people are strongly for or against one side.

One of my children had disastrous side effects from medication. He talked about suicide and did other harmful things like throwing himself into a tree, repeatedly. For him, a natural diet was enough.

But another one of my kids had great success with medication. His IQ jumped several points because it gave him a needed ability to focus. It also helped with impulse problems.

Sometimes medication can be helpful in certain situations, like when a child has to go to school. Maybe they don't need the extra focus when they aren't trying to study. No child should ever be medicated without a thorough investigation into what the child's real needs are. And medication should definitely never be used simply because teachers or parents can't handle him or her. They should only use it to help your child handle life.

Starting medication can be a difficult process. Sometimes it can take up to three months to find one that works, and in the meantime, it can feel as if your child is a guinea pig. Once you do find a medication that works, then you have to watch for changes.

When a child grows or goes into puberty, you might find you must change doses or types of medications. It's such a hard choice to make and requires careful, dedicated observation for the duration of the time.

With the extra work, either from adopting a natural diet or keeping tabs on medication, you're bound to encounter more than a little criticism. You might hear that you're a "health nut" because you don't let your son eat red dye or sugar. Or the other health nuts will tell you-you're poisoning your child with the chemical medication. Either way, you will once again find yourself defending your parenting skills; never an easy thing to do. But just remember-all that matters is your child's wellbeing. As long as you are making decisions that are best for him or her, then you are doing your job.

Going all natural

I experienced a lot of change when I went with an all-natural diet. My oldest son ate no dyes or preservatives for two years. He was one of the healthiest kids ever. The downside to eating natural is that pure food is expensive. It takes more time to prepare meals when everything has to be made from scratch.

I wish I could say I make my own bread with no dyes, and I never eat McDonald's, but I don't really make the time anymore. In fact, my youngest child has terrible eating habits. She has always been picky and is sensitive to certain textures. On top of that, she doesn't adapt well to change. She won't even eat red and green M&M's at Christmas because they are not the normal colors.

I learned with one of my other kids, who was also a picky eater that forcing him to eat was not the best route. Instead, I have my daughter try things here and there, slowly adding new things to her diet.

What is the big deal with labels?

My favorite movie of all time is *I Am Sam*. Sean Penn plays a mentally impaired father fighting the state for custody of his child. Michelle Pfeiffer is his lawyer. She says to him, "What do I call you? Retarded? Mentally impaired?" Sam's response is, "Just call me Sam."

I know how difficult it can be to hear the label for the first time. And I can't say it gets much easier to hear as your child gets older. But they need labels.

With my first son, I told an advocate I did not want a label for my child. Boy was I wrong. Labels are your legal key to get what you need from the school. Legally, they are not required to go above and beyond if you don't have a label.

If you disagree with a label that the school has given, get another opinion. I made the mistake of letting the school tell me that a pediatric psychologist was wrong and that I had wasted my money getting my child tested. I know now that my hunch was right, and if I hadn't succumbed to the school's opinion, maybe my son would have gotten more help.

It's important to know your rights and to be firm. A doctor's diagnosis can hold up in court. So follow your instincts and keep asking for help when you feel it's needed.

Labels are tricky. Even though they can garner the assistance you need, they are also not something that your child will want to carry with him as they get older. As Dr. Kevin Leman says in his book *Running the Rapids* (Tyndale House Publishers, 2005), a teenager's goal every day can sometimes be as simple as avoiding embarrassment. They will feel, no matter how much you praise them that being different is bad. It's only natural. Your child just wants to fit in.

Labels are touchy. You need to let your child know his label is important. You also need to teach them to become an advocate for themselves. For example, if your child knows it is on his IEP not to mark off for spelling, and a teacher does anyway, they need to learn how to respectfully address their teacher after class.

At one time in particular, Mike was struggling and the school felt they were doing all they could for a child with ADD. We took him to Dr. Zelkowitz for more testing, and they gave Mike a diagnosis of encephalopathy (a progressive degenerative brain disease) with ADD.

The school reacted so much more quickly and with real empathy. I was a little torn at the reaction. Though I was happy to get something more done for Mike, I also felt disappointed that one word inspired more reaction than five prior meetings where I asked for more help.

Facing reality

In a perfect world, Dad would be home by five-thirty and would help with homework, and then everyone would sit down to a calm meal. In the real world, Mom is trying to do homework while making dinner, dropping kids off at soccer practice, and changing the laundry. It becomes necessary to get creative and to improvise. I've taken flashcards in the vehicle and made it a game of seeing how many we can get done while waiting at red lights. Don't feel guilty when gets life is bogged down with so much to do. If you don't have a "Leave It to Beaver" home, you're normal. It's important to realize that you can still succeed through methods that aren't typical or "normal."

I once put in a balance beam in the backyard so that my kids could work on their balance while still having fun. I added a pull-up bar to the playroom, and now my six-year-old is always hanging upside down. It helps to use up some of her nonstop energy but also builds muscle. She has a hard time holding a pencil and strengthened muscle will help her handwriting skills.

It has concerned some parents that hanging upside down while watching TV is not safe. What if she falls? Yes, it's true, there is the risk she could fall, but all of my kids have been natural climbers. I figured it was wise to give them something that was meant to be climbed, instead of other things like dressers and countertops. When therapists have come into my house, their reactions have always been positive. One even commented that she wished other clients would consider the same thing.

If you can't hang a bar but want to work on building muscle in the hand, try having your child use small,

138

normal sized crayons instead of the larger ones. It's almost impossible to grasp a small crayon in the wrong way, but with the larger ones, there are many ways to hold it incorrectly.

I've also picked up stationery from garage sales and dollar stores and played mailman with my kids. Writing fake letters and adding lots of glitter and stickers makes practicing their handwriting fun. Working with learning-disabled children is all about improvisation and flexibility.

Chapter 23

Life in these fast-paced years of raising children can be hard enough without adding the extra concern and stress of parenting learning-disabled children. I read a book, *Married With Special-Needs Children* (Laura E. Marshak and Fran P. Prezant, Woodbine House, 2007), in which the authors quote studies showing that divorce rates are high in families with autism.

Similarly, Jenny McCarthy stated when she was on *The Oprah Winfrey Show* that the divorce statistics are as high as 85 to 90 percent in a family dealing with autism. They even quoted this same statistic in a presidential debate in 2008. If those numbers are accurate, they are astoundingly high!

I researched, trying to find the source of those studies, but most results showed that divorce rates were inconclusive. The closest one I could find which seemed to agree was from *Autism Weekly* (Brooch, et al., 2003) which showed that the divorce rate is 17 percent higher in the US and 10 percent higher in the UK. That is higher-but not as high as they conveyed it on Oprah's show. This goes to prove that you can't believe everything you hear on *Oprah* (or from other celebrities, shows, or magazines).

But one thing which I have found that studies consistently show is that the top three reasons cited for divorce in these situations are money, stress, and miscommunication. These seem to go hand in hand when dealing with children who have disabilities. Money goes for doctors and testing, not for date nights and dinners out. There is an added stress from all the extra doctor appointments and social difficulties because of others who don't understand or judge you. And it is harder to make time to communicate with each other when there is all the extra work of juggling appointments and the special needs of the children.

One mother of an ADD child said, "It is so exhausting every night having to keep a routine of forty-five minutes of ritual stuff to get my son to sleep. Many times my husband is asleep on the couch before I'm done putting my son to bed. So do I wake him up to have a little marriage fun or get the laundry done and let him sleep? Unfortunately, the peace of mind of getting the laundry done sounds pretty good-but that can really take the spark out of a marriage."

But even so, in the end, you don't want to become a statistic. Going through the struggles can strengthen you if you are willing to invest in your marriage. In the book *Married With Special-Needs Children*, the authors write about many marriage situations.

One of my favorite quotes is from a parent with a child who has fragile X syndrome. She says, "If you are in the middle of a storm and are fighting, don't whack the boat with an oar.

In the middle of a crisis, don't take away the support you have and beat at it-that would be dumb. You should love, nurture, and care for the person, or you will never get through the storm." You need to make your marriage a priority. It's vital that you work together to educate your kids. When we started school with our oldest, I did 99 percent of the homework and met with teachers and doctors on my own. My husband was willing to help more, but he was in school himself and was working over 40 hours a week.

I am embarrassed to say, but it took a doctor's test results to wake us up to what was going on with our son. When the doctor gave us feedback, John and I had two different reactions. I was like, "Yeah, that's my son all right," but John was in shock. I couldn't believe how little knowledge he had about our son's daily life. The doctor told us we needed to do more of this together.

We learned from that and aimed to do better at having John more involved. He tries as hard as he can to make it to IEP meetings, and when he can't, I try to discuss all the decisions with him.

This system means that sometimes we end up having important conversations at eleven o'clock at night. The conversations have to be had, and sometimes that's the first and only chance we have.

It's important to have the discussions when you and your spouse can have quiet time alone, away from the children, when you're not stressed at the moment. It doesn't happen often, to be honest; at least not for us.

My husband's job requires a lot of time, and he was in night school for about ten years. Then, factor in five children-time alone was not always an option. But we made the best of it.

A good, applicable verse from Proverbs again is "The beginning of strife is like releasing water; therefore, stop contempt before a quarrel starts."

To the fathers who are working very hard to pay the bills, I have a piece of advice. Next time your wife has had a stressful day, and it seems she has done nothing; don't just assume that she really has done nothing but twiddle her thumbs all day.

There have been days when I have barely been home to even think about making dinner because I've been running around to eye therapy and neurologist appointments, followed by two hours of homework that had to be completed for the next day.

It's important for husbands to understand all that goes into meeting the needs of your children. Patience is necessary, especially with parenting learning-disabled children. I always assumed I'd have a home like Beaver Cleaver's mom, with a nice dinner ready on the table when my one and only love of my life walks through the door.

But the reality comes closer to the mom from *Malcolm in the Middle*-harried and frenzied as I constantly rush to get everyone to the right appointments and meetings. It'd be ideal to have a spotless house-but as the husband, just be aware how truly impossible this can be on most days. It isn't that I don't try, but rather, I'm far too overwhelmed to make it a reality.

I still struggle with low self-esteem. I have a wonderful husband who is so understanding and loving, yet every once in a while, he gets upset with my forgetfulness or inability to organize and clean the house. I don't blame him. I can be a slob.

As I age and have to deal with added complications from hormonal mood swings, things can get a bit heated. Growing up, my parents never yelled. There was never a fight between them. John's parents, though, argued more.

When John and I fight and we say mean things, I have a very hard time getting over them. My mind plays tricks on me, and the devil attacks me right where I'm vulnerable.

I know very well that John would never leave me, yet I can begin to rationalize a million reasons about how I have finally let him down for the last time, and he's sick of me.

I then end up running through all of my faults and finish with my aging body, which is far from the younger, perkier woman whom John married. Trust me-as any woman can tell you-a woman's body can sag in places I never even thought of as a young girl.

I know the thoughts are wrong, and that it's the devil's goal to tear us apart, but sometimes it's difficult to make the cycle stop. I feel that much of this mind game stems from the experiences of having failed at learning so many times.

This is all part of the struggle with low self-esteem. I pray for my kids' future spouses-that they will be blessed with wives or husbands who will be as accepting of each other's faults as John has been with me.

I desire the perfect marriage for my children and myself, and I understand as much as anyone that making a marriage work comes from determination and loving each other for their faults and their strengths.

But none of it is possible without God's loving example. He loves me as I am and willingly died for me. Even though it feels as if I sometimes just barely stumble through here on earth, I know that He loves me and would die to save me all over again if He had to. It's true sacrificial love that redeems me and that also makes marriages last.

Making it work in the real world

"Before I was married, I had a hundred theories about raising children and no kids. Now I have children and no theories." John Wilmot. People have given me lots of practical advice over the years that sounds great in theory-but theory is not the real world. Suggestions like doing homework at the same time every day, in a quiet place, to establish a routine sound like they would be effective. But to put it simply-it's not always possible.

I don't know actual percentages, but it seems a lot of these homes that end up with split marriages are not because of the disability, but because it was one more issue added to a pile of things that weren't being worked through. It's difficult.

Not only do you have the added level of financial stress unless you're fortunate enough to have a full-coverage insurance, but all the extra appointments as well. All of it stacks up to adding more of a burden to the marriage, even in the best-case scenarios.

There will always be more decisions to make, which will mean more opportunities to disagree. It's frustrating for me when I've been working one way for months and John comes home one day and tells me a better way to go about it. In those circumstances, I get defensive easily.

It's exhausting to spend three hours a night doing homework. So often when he gets home, I am very spent. It's hard to find alone time, and sometimes when life is so busy between juggling everything, it's easy to forget how much fun your spouse is. It may seem impossible but make time to talk-and not about the kids. Talk about the two of you. But don't spend that precious time debating whose day was harder.

Governmental research shows that fathers are only half as likely to be involved in their child's special education program as compared to regular education. This was from a US Department of Education study done in 1997.

It's a tragic fact that dads often feel they are less needed, or simply aren't interested in taking an active role in the life of their special-needs child. If anything, Dad's involvement is more critical.

I have talked to many couples who express that the dad feels hurt because he doesn't have the football playing son he always expected, or that he won't be able to play catch with his son like he always dreamed of. And sadly, many fathers leave the family because of their own disillusionment.

We recently had a father-son camp out at our church. John came home feeling beat. It wasn't the hiking or sleeping on the hard ground that got him, but the realization of how much help our son required.

Yes, he requires more than the average kid to do the simplest things. Our son wanted to do his badges on his own but couldn't read or write at the proper level. Some other parents had little patience with his attempts. It's difficult having a child who others look at oddly.

My son struggled to get along with the other boys. My son's best friend was along. However, even as a best friend, the boy was still just 11 years old and told my son he only wanted to be friends with him when they were at home-not when others were around. It was very hard for John and I know what it's like; I've been through that many times, so I felt for him.

Yet the other part of me was upset with John. How did he not realize this sooner? I've read that children are part of the mother, but just an extended part of the dad. I can get overly protective of the kids, even with their father. I know that it's wrong, but it's a reality. It can tear us apart if we let it. The kids see it too, and if they can, will use it to their advantage. Kids are smart.

A lot of mothers who I've talked to while writing this book have told me negative stories about marriage. It can be so hard. Yet I talked to one woman who doesn't feel overwhelmed with the thought she will have to be responsible to take care of and pay for the care of her two handicapped children as long as they are around.

She and her husband were married later in life and had their years of "freedom." So she and her husband find the reality of caring for their children as part of God's plan to keep their later years as full of life as their younger years were.

Another family said they had three boys in three years, so they were too busy to fight about their sons' education. They said it made their marriage stronger in many ways because they stayed at home a lot to make it easy on their son. Facing these situations is not often portrayed in a positive light, but these two couples were refreshing to hear. It's all about perspective.

Another couple told me they would have split up if it weren't for God and the fact they had waited to marry until they were older. They both felt if they had been younger, they may not have been mature enough to deal with the extra stress.

Siblings

We all know sisters and brothers can fight. Kids will always want the attention of their mom and dad. It's hard to balance that in a "normal" setting-it's even more difficult when some children require a larger amount of attention to simply make it through each day.

Personalities work for and against each other. One time I said to my daughter who has no learning disabilities, "Sometimes I feel bad that our life is so crazy-that I spend so much time doing homework with your brothers. Do you feel left out?" Her response? "Are you kidding-I'm happy.

We don't have a boring house where everyone's on the couch watching TV by eight o'clock." I'm sure she meant what she said, but I know that sometimes she felt set aside. She is a very driven girl, an overachiever even. I'm sure that most of the school can't figure out how she fits into our family. I think her drive is one thing that makes her great. But she is also compassionate and looks out for others.

A few people have commented that she is driven because it's the only way she can get attention from John and me. I hope that's not true. I feel she was born with the will to compete and we just encourage it because it's one of her strengths. I feel even when she was in the womb, she had an extra kick. One day she came home from school, upset at something a teacher had said to the class. It even was her favorite teacher that year. The class had been complaining about too much homework, and the teacher said, "If you can't finish your homework in less than 30 minutes, then you're stupid."

My daughter, Jean, said the teacher clearly didn't know that one of her classmates took twenty minutes just to focus enough to write his name. Jean had also watched her brother's work for hours on just a few sentences. She had become very compassionate and understood that those difficulties had nothing to do with their actual intelligence.

I got a chance to discuss that teacher's comment with her later in the year. It surprised the teacher at the thoughtfulness of Jean and apologetically said sometimes teachers speak out of frustration. I said, "I know the feeling-parents speak out of frustration at times, too."

Jean is actually planning on being a teacher. She will be better off from the experiences she's had at home, watching her siblings struggle just to achieve what so many take for granted.

But Jean isn't the only one who's driven. My other kids are as well, in their own ways. When they put their minds to do something, they really give it their all. The only difference is that it's not obvious to everyone else. No one can really comprehend how much effort it takes for my dyslexic child to read at the level he's at.

There will be other people who may are confused at how

different your children are. One time an adult said, right in front of my son and daughter, "Jean, you must be adopted-how else can you be related to such a spacey brother?"

This person didn't mean harm but was just ignorant with learning disabilities. I've had people make the same sort of statements about me. Ignorance can be quite hurtful though. It's hard enough to raise teenagers to be spiritually grounded people. It would help if other adults would show respect and not shoot their mouths off without realizing the consequences of their uninformed words.

Sometimes, as a parent, you must step in and let other adults know certain comments are inappropriate, preferably not while your child is around. It's unrealistic to expect that everyone will understand what you're working with, but for those who refuse, the only thing to do is to pray for them. Assigning blame and being offended will do no good for you or your family.

It's difficult as it is to be fair to each child since they are all so different. Fairness does not mean equal. An analogy from a video I saw once compared fairness to this: If you had a room full of children, and one had an asthma attack, you give the suffering child an inhaler. Is it unfair that the rest of the class didn't get inhalers too? Of course not. As parents, we need to give each child what they need to succeed.

Perhaps one child doesn't need much help with her homework, but another does. The first child might feel that it's unfair that she doesn't get the same amount of time spent with you. She may want you to read her a longer bedtime story or spend extra time with her doing a different activity. There is no easy answer for how to make sure that each child feels loved. It's a balancing act, to be sure, but through prayer and discernment, it's possible to ensure that each child gets the fair amount of attention she needs.

Isaac and Rachel are a biblical example of what happens when parental attention gets out of whack. That married couple manipulated, lie, and cheat to get their favorite child just what he wanted. Not the best idea if a couple wants to maintain a strong marriage.

Another example of favoritism gone wrong was with Joseph and his brothers. Jacob's bias with his son actually tore the family apart. That's not to say those parenting children which are completely opposite isn't a challenge. It is. Parents need to work daily at meeting all of their needs-and it can be quite a task when children are as different as night and day.

It's important to make sure that the other children in a family understand that learning disabilities are real. They should also be asked to help. It makes the other kids have a better comprehension of what their siblings are going through. For example, why not have them read stories together? In today's society, it's easy to forget that families are supposed to help each other-not be splintered and divided.

After they made Jean prom queen, someone said: "Well, isn't it nice to be vindicated that you have a daughter who the school is proud of-and who you can be proud of." Well of course I'm proud of my daughter's accomplishments. She is a strong Christian witness to many people.

In fact, even the night they crowned her was a witnessing moment. She had originally asked for them to withdraw her name from the choices because the theme of the night was offensive to her God. She did all of this behind the scenes, but we asked the school to change the theme, feeling it was not fair to Jean. Why should she step out of the running for something that she had been involved with for four years in a row? The school understood our side and changed the theme.

So yes, of course, I was incredibly proud of Jean. But what others fail to realize is that I am just as proud of my other children, I need not be vindicated in the eyes of the town or the school. I consider all of my children equal blessings because God saw fit to give each of them to me. And He doesn't make mistakes.

Sometimes, siblings can be cruel to each other. They can make fun of their weaknesses as can happen in most families. For example, I have tried to be careful to have my kids do their homework separately so that my older son doesn't feel bad that his little sister can read more words than he does. It's important to make sure that siblings and friends understand the disabilities too.

But most parents feel as if sibling relationships, (when disabilities are involved), are very similar to those without disabilities. Kids fight, or as one mom put it, "beat the tar out of each other whether or not there is a disability."

The disability can add embarrassment and change the way you do some things as a family, but ultimately, it's up to the parents to monitor how these relationships will turn out.

Chapter 24

I hate the words "smart" and "intelligent". What exactly do they mean? The dictionary defines the word "smart" as an adjective that means "causing keen pain," and secondly as "intense pain." The third definition is "alert, clever, and capable." None of the definitions have to do with grades or school. Yet where do we hear the word the most? At school, well, now who's smart? We don't even use the word in the proper context most of the time.

A doctor can have an IQ of 130 and invent the cure for heart disease, yet that very same doctor might smoke three packs of cigarettes a day. In that instance, is his high IQ really doing him justice? How can smart be defined in that instance?

I understand the need for IQ's, especially as it applies to labeling a child so they can get the help they need. I think they make too much of the IQ most of the time It comes from a standardized test. What about those who don't do well at test-taking?

Those who have short attention spans or can't read well will struggle. Does that automatically mean that their IQ's are less? A written test can't prove it in this case.

There are so many variables that can affect the results of written tests. I once took an IQ test that used southern jargon, but I live near Chicago. I was clueless. The wording was in the English language, but the phraseology was beyond my comprehension. Did that automatically mean I wasn't as smart as those who live in the southern dialectal region simply because they knew what the questions were asking and I didn't?

Another girl in my class had spent her summers in the south, so she knew what "grits" were. Was that the determining factor between her IQ and mine? Sometimes I feel that these tests show nothing about intellect or intelligence but reveal certain levels of ignorance.

I once heard a speaker say it appalled her at how people would throw the word IQ around when speaking in front of her mentally impaired sister. She wanted to challenge these people, ask them if they even knew what their own IQ's were. Most people don't actually but are quick to make judgments when they know someone else's and it is lower than average. What is "average" anyway?

Howard Gardner (*Intelligence Reframed: Multiple Intelligences for the 21st Century, Peruses Distribution, November 2000*) has a theory that there are eight different kinds of intelligence: linguistic, logical-mathematical, spatial, bodily kinesthetic, musical, interpersonal, intrapersonal, and naturalist.

Linguistic pertains to the comprehension of the written word (i.e. William Shakespeare). Logical-mathematical refers to mathematical computation and deductive reasoning (i.e. Isaac Newton). Spatial refers to balance and the ability to accurately perceive, recognize, manipulate, modify, and transform shape, form, and matter (i.e. Leonardo da Vinci). Bodily kinesthetic means an ability to orchestrate body control, handle objects, and skillfully perform tasks (i.e. Tiger Woods). Musical covers areas such as pitch, melody, texture, themes, and harmony (i.e. Wolfgang Amadeus Mozart). Interpersonal deals with the ability to inspire and instruct through emotions and opinion (i.e. Virginia Woolf). Intrapersonal covers areas of knowledge and understanding where one's strength is in motivation and self-oriented success (i.e. Oprah Winfrey). Naturalist refers to being able to discriminate between category differences and species in the natural world (i.e. Charles Darwin).

Intelligence is not limited to school "smarts," and I think it's important we continue to work to change the definitions and assumptions. Learning-disabled children are just as gifted as others-their gifts are just manifested in different ways.

How many of the above examples would have had incredibly high IQ's? Maybe they all would have, or maybe some would have been average, or below. Either way, their accomplishments were not measured by IQ numbers, and today, that's not what society remembers these people by.

Ultimately, it's important to find what your child is gifted at and to praise it. God chose to use many kinds of people throughout the Bible-low, high, and everywhere in between. What matters is a humility and willingness to serve, not an extraordinary amount of intelligence and wit. It's clear with Moses. He was living in Pharaoh's house, ruling as a prince of Egypt-a world power of the day. Yet it wasn't until Moses had been exiled from that country, and was found wandering in the wilderness, that God called him into action.

Israel chose strong, handsome, gifted Saul for their king, yet he wasn't God's preferred man for the job. God anointed David, a humble shepherd boy, for the task of ruling his people with His blessing. Let your children know God will use them too, in ways they'll never be able to imagine if they will respond to his desires for their lives.

The prophet Isaiah prayed a bold prayer 6:8: "Send me." That's it. Not "send me somewhere warm," or "send me someplace comfortable." Just "send me." It's a daring thing to pray because we don't know how it will turn out. We need to teach our children to pray this way as well.

Trust that God has given them gifts He will use for great and unseen purposes. He has plans for them which He has known of since before the dawn of time-don't think He will fail to come through for them, or that somehow, your child is the only one whose life will be a flop. God doesn't orchestrate mistakes.

It can be tricky though; to navigate the path of praising a child's gift without making him feel proud. It's also important to remember that just because they are good at one thing doesn't mean they need not improve other areas that need strengthening.

For example, if your child wears the same type of pants every day, let them. There are bigger things to worry about. But you need to explain to your child the importance of cleanliness and first impressions. You need to help your child understand things they might miss by pointing out that which might not occur to them. For example, things such as clean clothes can make a big difference at job interviews.

Why care?

We know that God loves children. The words child or children are in the Bible over 600 times. Jesus definitely made children a priority. In Matthew 19:14 he said, "Let the little children come to me."

Our country had our eyes opened after the horror of the Columbine shootings. The revenge those boys took may have been a first for our country, but the story of cruelty, low self-esteem, and the desire to belong was not. The desire to belong is in all of us.

Learning-disabled children are at a greater risk of having to deal with depression and suicide. They also more commonly turn to drugs and gangs. We need to be there to meet the needs of the kids who are struggling and know of those around them who are being cruel. We need to show love where it hasn't been given and truly be Christ like to those who are in pain and suffering.

Dr. Nancy Cowardin did a study of learning and emotionally disabled teens after high school. They arrest thirty-one percent of learning-disabled and fifty-seven percent of by the time they have been out of school for five years.

Some of this may be in part because they are missing key social skills or aren't able to charm their way out of an arrest. Either way, it's a dramatically high number.

We can see the effects on the criminal justice system. It affects our budgets through higher taxes. The same study also found an average deficit of 7 to 9 IQ points that transcend controls of age, race, gender, and socioeconomic status. This discrepancy mirrors that of the learning-disabled population.

Chapter 25

It was difficult for me to pull my children out of the Christian school they had been attending. I believed strongly in the curriculum, but they weren't able to offer the help that the public school could.

A Christian school should produce a self-sufficient, well-educated, God-centered student. The goal is that they go into the world with an aim to put God first. In contrast, a public school aims to produce a self-sufficient, well-educated, American citizen who helps others by his own success.

We transferred our kids to the public school, which is great, but it went against my own personal desires for my children. It turned out, however, that God used the one thing that went against what I wanted to provide my kids with the help they needed.

There is also the option of homeschooling. While we were living overseas, I taught my kids at home. It can be very enjoyable, but it takes a huge amount of commitment and time.

The method of education you choose is a huge decision. No matter which way you decide to educate your children, you need to be involved in the process.

Chapter 26

I think it's a good idea to look back over some humorous experiences we've had over the years. Keeping a light-hearted point of view can be important and encouraging-it helps to balance out the days that feel overwhelming and impossible.

Here are some of our funny incidents and ones from people we know:

My ten-year-old who can't read came home on Valentine's Day so excited because he'd made, cards for my husband and me. He gave me mine first-it was a chicken made out of a heart. I love chickens, and he knew that.

The teacher told him he should give that one to his dad, but he said, "I knew you would want this one, Mom. Three hours later, John came home and my son ran to get the card for him. John opened it and read, "World's Greatest Mom."

To this, my son replied: "Oh, so that's why my teacher wanted Mom to have it."

Another time I had a meeting with one of my son's teachers. She was worried about my son's lack of self-esteem. I replied, "No self-esteem? He wore a pink Energizer bunny costume, which he made himself, for Halloween. How much self-esteem do you need to wear a pink bunny outfit?"

When I was a child, my mom thought of a great way for me to practice my writing skills. She knew my class at school was in a tie for first place in the competition to see who could collect the most of Campbell's soup labels.

She had me remove all the labels off our cans at home. In their place, I wrote the names of each soup on a piece of paper and taped it to the cans.

To get the full impact of this story, you have to understand that I came from a family of six kids. I had to write about 200 new labels for soup cans. The only real problem was that no one, including myself, could read what I wrote. My poor dad ate surprise soup for about a year.

I talked to the parent of an autistic child was around 13 years old. He could stay home alone. The only thing was that he didn't do very well was comprehending others when they talked, so his parents told him never to answer the door, and if he answered the phone, he was to say that Mom or Dad was in the shower.

Well, he received a phone call and told the caller Mom and Dad were in the shower. Later that night when the parents got to the Boy Scout meeting, all the leaders laughed and said, "Well, now we know why you two were late."

I heard a parent refer to ADHD as the "Oh look! Something shiny disorder!" I laughed. It seemed like a better name.

A mother told me a story about her son when he was four years old. He had climbed up and changed the time on her clock because she had said: "When the big hand is on the six, we will leave to go." So he changed the clock back so they would never leave to go to the doctors. They ended up being late.

Another mother had a story about a wedding experience. Her two boys were asked to be in a wedding. She was so excited. Her girlfriend who was getting married was a special needs teacher, so she was well aware of the task that she was asking of the boys.

The oldest was five and the youngest was four and happened to be ADHD and OCD. The wedding was at an old farmhouse. The wedding party was supposed to walk over some beautiful bridges before reaching the party. They made it over the first bridge, but the second differed from the first. The four-year-old thought that throwing dirt into the water would be much more fun. His dad grabbed him and carried a not-so-happy four-year-old to the front, where the minister was standing.

Then the bride walked up the aisle-such a pretty picture on her dad's arm-until the four-year-old bolted down the aisle to get back to that bridge. He ran right through the bride and her father, splitting their embrace. The bride ended up laughing so hard that she could barely speak. I said, "That must have been a great photo." The mom said, "Oh-the pictures were good, but the video was even better."

Another story came from a mother who had a young son with a cognitive delay. One wonderful Sunday morning her son was sitting in front of the church for the children's sermon. He was literally holding his mouth shut with his hand, bouncing up and down, desperately wanting to say something.

Finally, the minister said, "Yes-do you have something to share?" He said, "Yes! Guess what I found! A hair on my private parts! At first, I thought it was my mom's because it was dark. I thought it fell on me in the shower because she showered first, but nope, Mom said it needed to stay there. It is my first big boy hair." That mom slithered down her pew and out the door. Talk about utterly embarrassing-but truly something she would never forget. Kids say the darndest things, for sure.

If you think about it, I bet you can come up with a few of these stories yourself. Share them with each other; laugh a little. My next goal is to compile a collection of others' funny stories. Life can be stressful, but finding the simple amusements in daily living can mean the difference between being overwhelmed and knowing that you're going to make it through to the next day.

Epilogue

My son Mike wrote and delivered this speech earlier this year. I wanted to share it with you:

My name is Mike. I came to Elim two years ago because I could not read. At my old school, the kids would use me and make fun of me behind my back. But I know that God made me with these struggles so that I could learn to be a hard worker and finish the things I start. I know God has a purpose for my life.

The song we are going to sing is called "I'll Always Stand for You." There is a line about how I have felt what it feels like to be rejected. All of us in our room know what it feels like to be rejected, mostly by people we thought were our friends. But no matter what, Jesus is always there for us. He was rejected by people too and knows how we sometimes feel.

I will always stand for Jesus. I will not back down from loving Him and talking about Him because Jesus is always on my side and I know He would never back down from me. I am a Christian. And by the way, I just read this whole thing to you. God is good.

Made in the USA
Columbia, SC
24 June 2019